D0526999

THE ROAD TO WIGAN PIER REVISITED

Essex County Council

3013020235475 8

THE ROAD TO WIGAN PIER REVISITED

Stephen Armstrong

CONSTABLE • LONDON

Constable & Robinson Ltd
55–56 Russell Square
London WC1B 4HP
www.constablerobinson.com

First published in the UK by Constable,
an imprint of Constable & Robinson Ltd, 2012

Copyright © Stephen Armstrong, 2012

The right of Stephen Armstrong
to be identified as the author of this
work has been asserted by him in accordance with the
Copyright, Designs and Patents Act 1988

All rights reserved. This book is sold subject to the condition
that it shall not, by way of trade or otherwise, be lent, re-sold,
hired out or otherwise circulated in any form of binding or cover
other than that in which it is published and without a similar
condition including this condition being imposed on the
subsequent purchaser.

A copy of the British Library Cataloguing in
Publication data is available from the British Library

ISBN: 978-1-78033-691-6

Printed and bound in the UK

1 3 5 7 9 10 8 6 4 2

For Lyndsey Cameron Armstrong
and Mohayuddin Qazi

Contents

Acknowledgements

Cat Ledger, for making this happen; Undaleeb Qazi – by rights her name should also be on the cover; Robin Foxon in Wigan and Joe McEvory in Bradford, two excellent researchers; Sarah Dransfield at Oxfam for all her help, advice and encouragement, and everyone else at Oxfam; Helen Barnard at the Joseph Rowntree Foundation; Toby Lloyd and Bill Rashleigh at Shelter; Eileen Daveny in Speke; Joe and Brian G. in Manchester; Andy, Tarby and Ken Barlow in Wigan; Shaun Noble; Yvonne Edge at the Pankhurst Centre; Alex Bennett and Anna Rothery in Liverpool; Stuart Speeden at Edge Hill University; Ash in Sheffield; Wilf Sullivan at the TUC; Karen Chouhan at Equanomics; Mike Quiggin in Bradford; Gordon Bowker; Geoffery Shryhane at the Wigan Observer; Simon Woolley at OBV, Nathan Lewis, Jess Wheatley and Maria Bogers;

Leo Hollis and Andreas Campomar at Constable & Robinson for saving everything; Ryan Davies and Simon Pethwick for starting it; Howard Watson for tidying it up; Helen Hawkins for my career; Anna Nicoll and Hannah Pullen at HBO for all their help; Bob Kelsey, Richard Benson, Will Hodgkinson, Richard Cook and Britta Jaschinski; 'London Calling' by the Clash; Mum, Dad and Matt for brilliance in a troubled year; Ken and Jill Coles for exceptional kindness and care; finally, and most importantly, to Rosa, Tess and Georgia for everything.

Introduction

On 5 August 2011, the Friday before the riots broke out in Tottenham, I had a long conversation with a man from the Dearne Valley in South Yorkshire – a once fertile coal seam, now one of the most deprived parts of the UK. For years after the mines closed nothing had been done to relieve the misery except a few hand-wringing reports from academics amazed to discover that heroin had arrived in former pit villages, he told me. He went on to describe the blocked views, the bulldozed homes, the forced job losses, the roads over football pitches, the long-term unemployment unrelieved by anything other than temporary schemes and a growing perception outside the Dearne Valley that the current residents' terrible situation is somehow partly their fault.

'There's a sense that the white working class is not

being listened to that groups like the BNP and the EDL tap into,' this man explained, referring to the rise of the popularity of the British National Party and the English Defence League. 'Politicians don't seem sure how to deal with it – cut down immigration is the only answer. But that's not the core reason. That's not really why people are angry. People want to be respected. They don't like being ignored. Over the last thirty years it's been lots of little things, little jabs and cuts, that combine to make a big thing – this sense, with nothing to contradict you, that nobody cares what you say. I don't know why people aren't rioting.'

The following night's chaos was no surprise to some. In June, for instance, Chief Superintendent Keith Hunter of Humberside Police had warned: 'people are being made redundant, unemployment is going up, offenders aren't going to prison for as long and the probation service has been slashed. The police service is being cut so our ability to catch people and lock them up is affected. People can make their own judgement about what is likely to happen because of that.'

For others – especially the media industry – the riots were a shocking surprise. In groping for answers, George Orwell's name came up again and again – quoted by those condemning and those defending the rioters in equal measure, from the BBC to the website of Canada's foreign policy council, Citizenship and Immigration Canada – referencing everything from

1984 to his journalism but, of course, coming back again and again to *The Road to Wigan Pier*, his impassioned account of three months documenting the living conditions of the unemployed and the working class in the industrial north of England during the Depression of the 1930s.

The parallels are obvious – Orwell headed north in February 1936 as the UK struggled in the grip of a long double-dip recession. The 1929 stock market crash shut off the supply of American credit to a world deeply in hock after spending heavily during the First World War. The crash caught the Labour government by surprise and it lost power to a Conservative-dominated coalition that set about extensive budget cuts and welfare reform.

All the same, there are many other documents of the time – from Seebohm Rowntree's 1936 survey of poverty in York to A.J. Cronin's novel set in a mining community, *The Stars Look Down* (1935), hailed at the time for its realism and later to inspire the film *Billy Elliot*. Rowntree's report is certainly better researched; A.J. Cronin – the doctor turned novelist whose work inspired Labour's Aneurin Bevan – draws beautiful characters and offers an epic sweep. So how can *The Road to Wigan Pier*, a slim, hastily researched piece of reportage, still have such resonance that, seventy-five years after publication, the *Daily Telegraph* should urge its readers to buy a copy in 2009, 2010 and 2011 – all in opinion pieces by different small 'c' conservative writers? Because it's Orwell and because it's terrifyingly appropriate today.

Why does Orwell still matter so much? Perhaps it's because, in fighting in the Spanish Civil War, he was a writer who acted on his beliefs. Perhaps it's because he was the arch contrarian and so, since his death in 1950, he has gradually become a secular saint, a touchstone for the political left and right alike and a point of reference for taking a critical stance on almost anything. In the United States, the battle over healthcare reform had the Tea Party quoting at length from *1984*, convinced that Barack Obama was Big Brother, whilst the BNP quoted Orwell in its defence of David Starkey's attacks on immigration. On the left, everyone from John Pilger to anarchists find comfort and encouragement in Orwell's words. In Sheffield, I came across an ex-steelworker with two tattoos – one of the white rose of Yorkshire and one of Orwell's face. He's not alone. Google 'Orwell tattoo' and see what you find.

John le Carré, at the opening of his recent novel, *Our Kind of Traitor* (2010), sends his protagonist Peregrine spinning from the cloistered walls of Oxbridge academia after he delivers a series of lectures called 'A Stifled Britain' in which he asks: 'Would Orwell have believed it possible that the same overfed voices which had haunted him in the 1930s, the same crippling incompetence, addictions to foreign wars and assumptions of entitlement were happily in place in 2009?'

Receiving no response from the blank student faces staring up at him, le Carré's protagonist provides the answer himself: 'no, Orwell would emphatically not have believed it. Or if he had he would have taken to the streets. He would have smashed some serious glass.'

Across the political divide, August 2011 saw Peter Oborne, chief political correspondent for the *Telegraph*, comparing rioters with politicians and seeing Orwell's pigs from *Animal Farm* (1945) standing in the House of Commons when he wrote:

> I believe that the criminality in our streets cannot be dissociated from the moral disintegration in the highest ranks of modern British society. It has become acceptable for our politicians to lie and to cheat. An almost universal culture of selfishness and greed has grown up. Our politicians – standing sanctimoniously on their hind legs in the Commons – have shown themselves prepared to ignore common decency and, in some cases, to break the law.
>
> Certainly, the so-called feral youth seem oblivious to decency and morality. But so are the venal rich and powerful – too many of our bankers, footballers, wealthy businessmen and politicians. But the rioters have this defence: they

are just following the example set by senior and respected figures in society.

Something has gone horribly wrong in Britain. If we are ever to confront the problems which have been exposed in the past week, it is essential to bear in mind that they do not only exist in inner-city housing estates.

The culture of greed and impunity we are witnessing on our TV screens stretches right up into corporate boardrooms and the Cabinet. It embraces the police and large parts of our media. It is not just its damaged youth, but Britain itself that needs a moral reformation.

If it was Orwell's novels that gave him immortality, he himself insisted that what he most wanted to do was make political writing into an art. His starting point, he wrote, was 'because there is some lie that I want to expose, some fact to which I want to draw attention, and my initial concern is to get a hearing'. After reading *Homage to Catalonia* (1938), one critic took issue with Orwell's factual prose in a particular chapter: 'You've turned what might have been a good book into journalism,' the critic huffed. Orwell's response was simple: 'What he said was true, but I could not have done otherwise' – *The Road to Wigan Pier* is, likewise, a brilliant piece of journalism.

Orwell arrived in Wigan on a cold Saturday morning

early in February 1936, commissioned by his publisher Victor Gollancz to write about the conditions of the unemployed but finding himself drawn as much to the privations of miners, dockers and steelworkers who still clung to their jobs. Between January and March 1936 he visited Wigan, Barnsley and Sheffield and produced a passionate polemic that helped fuel the debate on poverty and responsibility, and ultimately helped lead to the development of the welfare state.

Following his path isn't a new idea. The journalist Bea Campbell did the same in 1981 in *Wigan Pier Revisited*. In 2011, both the BBC and the *Observer* sent reporters on the same road. All the same, seventy-five years on it seemed worthwhile to visit the grandchildren of the families Orwell had known, to see what had changed for the better and what had changed for the worse.

In some ways, we are living in bleaker times than 1936. Then, the unemployment rate was falling slowly from its 1932–3 peak of over 22 per cent. Although this figure seems incomparably high, in numerical terms this meant 2.23 million unemployed in January 1936, down from 2.98 million in January 1933. Today, unemployment is rising – in November 2011 it stood at 2.62 million, or 8.3 per cent. According to the House of Commons library, government changes to the way unemployment rates are measured over the past thirty years mean that 1933's 2.9 million unemployed as measured by today's standards hovered at just below 10 per cent.

Then there's leadership. When Orwell started out, the coalition prime minister was Stanley Baldwin who, in 1919, had donated one-fifth of his personal wealth to the Treasury to help pay off the national debt and try to create jobs. Compare this to the MPs' expenses scandal – Anthony Steen claimed £87,000 for the upkeep of his country house. Brian Binley claimed £57,000 for rent he paid to his own company. Sir Menzies Campbell had the taxpayer fork out £10,000 to redesign his flat in London, including a new king-size bed, scatter cushions and a plasma screen TV. In total, seventy MPs were implicated, helping themselves to hundreds of thousands of pounds worth of taxpayers' money. The idea that MPs would help pay off the national debt from their own purse seems like an insane fantasy. For Orwell it was recent history.

Instead, we're the ones paying through vicious cuts. In 2011 the Child Trust Fund was abolished, child benefit frozen, pension credits frozen, maternity grants cut. In the autumn, the winter fuel allowance was slashed – as fuel bills soar – proving potentially fatal for the elderly. In January 2012, people under thirty-five stopped receiving housing benefit unless they're living in a shared house. No more one-bedroom flats for junkies withdrawing and trying to avoid mates who still use. From April 2012, tax credits are being reduced and disability benefit withdrawn from one in five people. Although it's not until 2015 that the pension cuts really hit.

We already spend the lowest percentage in Europe of our GDP on the public sector and by 2015 we will be spending less than the United States. We've become the NeoCon poster boy. The voices for change are muted, drowned out by the hypocritical yells of indignation from an establishment that is almost entirely to blame for the wreckage we're trying to fix.

According to Sarah Dransfield at Oxfam GB, commenting on Orwell's *The Road to Wigan Pier*:

Many parts of the book are exactly the same as what we hear from people living in poverty today. People living four to a room or even 'hot bedding' if they are shift workers is common nowadays, especially with exploited migrant workers, whose lives are the same as the miners in Orwell's book. They often have travel-time deducted from their wages and costs such as safety equipment. Employers, particularly in the construction industry, often flout health and safety, like the mine-owners in the 1930s, and there's real job insecurity. Orwell talks about the hidden people in poverty, those who are working, but not on a 'living wage'. Over six million people in the UK are living in poverty and are working.

August 2011 figures from the Office for National Statistics showed more than 20 per cent of sixteen to twenty-four year-olds were unemployed and 100,000 had been on the dole for two years or more. Earlier in the year, the first full comparison of numbers from local authorities showed that men and women in Manchester, Liverpool and Blackburn die ten years younger than men and women living in Kensington and Chelsea.

Those figures are a little conceptual – so let's personalize the reduced average life expectancy of ten years. On one afternoon in August 2011 I met, amongst others, two people from an estate in Bradford, the Canterbury Estate, who were both around fifty and who weren't going to make it to fifty-five – cancer and cirrhosis respectively. Statistically, the chance that these two middle-aged, unemployed Brits would be smokers is about average for the UK while the chance that they'll be heavy drinkers is less likely. Generally, the poorer you are the less alcohol you drink. The chance that these two things will kill you, however, is much, much higher the poorer you are.

According to the Marmot Review (*Fair Society, Healthy Lives: A Strategic Review of Health Inequalities in England Post-2010*) – a huge study of the effects of poverty on health published in 2010 and updated in 2011 – the richer you are the more likely you are to drink heavily. The poorer you are, the more likely it is that drinking will kill you. It's the same with smoking. Poor people are damaged with greater intensity by each individual cigarette than the wealthy. Research from the 2002 health survey for England found the poorest smokers sucking an average 30 per cent more of the drug from each cigarette than the most affluent smokers – partly due to the poor smoking more, but also due to the intensity with which each cigarette was smoked. The less money you have, the harder you suck as much poison as possible from the crumpled white stick.

Both these dying Bradfordians were battling poverty. Both were parents. Neither of them asked for sympathy – they were proud, proud people. Unrelated, they were like chalk and cheese. She wept for the loss of her son; he bounded like the energizer bunny and grinned like a kid the whole time we talked. They knew they were under a sentence of death but they didn't complain, not once.

These are not exceptional scenarios or unusual stories. I met at least ten people who, in the first eight months of 2011, had been left with no money for almost a week, thanks to attempts to meet benefit reduction targets at Job Centres. This doesn't mean they only had a handful of change or subsistence money – they had not a single penny. In some cases, as you'll see, the results were so awful you can revive the phrase 'a fate worse than death' and understand what it means.

In August, we started to see the effects of living without a future. Whatever the specific personal reasons for people rioting across the country in early August – anger, frustration, personal gain or just the thrill – the vast majority of those arrested had one thing in common: they had absolutely no investment in society. They had no future to throw away.

This book retraces Orwell's steps in spirit, rather than as an exact facsimile, to find out why – sixty years after we were supposed to have made poverty history – a generation of people may have so little invested in the status quo that smashing things up seems a feasible option to suggest to your mates on Facebook.

However, even if I had Orwell's talent, *The Road to Wigan Pier* would be a complicated book to revisit. Almost everyone who's read Orwell has heard of it – it's fame far outranks *Burmese Days*, *A Clergyman's Daughter* and *Coming Up for Air*, and in the UK it probably beats *Keep the Aspidistra Flying*, *Homage to Catalonia* and possibly *Down and Out in Paris and London*. It's not quite up there with *1984* and *Animal Farm* in every part of the country, but it ranks alongside them for most people born to the north of Letchworth Garden City.

To make this task easier, I'm following the chapter plan for Orwell's original. His *Road to Wigan Pier* is divided into two parts – for the first seven chapters, Orwell walks the land, amongst the dark satanic mills. Chapter one is the life of the Brookers, a northern working-class family; chapter two is about the life of miners and conditions down a coal mine; chapter three looks at hygiene and money; chapter four tackles housing; chapter five is on unemployment; chapter six deals with food and health; and chapter seven is a rant about how ugly the towns are.

Part two could be subtitled 'What is to be done?' Compared to the clear-eyed description and detail of the first part, the second part of *The Road to Wigan Pier* was at the time of publication – and is still today – the part that more people dislike. It's one thing to read descriptions of miserable lives from a distance, to nod sadly and think 'how horrible'. It's a different thing entirely to have Orwell insist on a sweeping change that would resolve the problems. On the one hand, he discusses his solutions and why they may or may not appeal to the general population. On the other, he launches a series of attacks on the liberal left-leaning intelligentsia – picking out, amongst others, vegetarians, nudists, *New Statesman* readers and people who have beards or wear sandals.

Victor Gollancz refused to print this part of the book, sending out only the observation and critique. Later editions included everything. Reading reviews – even those published in 2008 by shocked American readers who came to Orwell believing he despised the state in all things, only to discover the author praising socialism – you can tell that Orwell setting out his beliefs, as opposed to mocking or condemning, sits uneasily with many of his fans.

After *The Road to Wigan Pier* he travelled to Spain to fight Franco, returning to pen *The Lion and the Unicorn: Socialism and the English Genius* – the book that, according to Danny Dorling, professor of human geography at the University of Sheffield and author of *So You Think You Know About Britain*, Orwell used to try and persuade Tories to vote Labour.

He wrote as bombs fell on London and as Britain put aside its politicking to deal with a disastrous emergency. Ultimately this book argues that we need similar unprecedented action today. As Peter Oborne argued, 'something has gone horribly wrong in Britain'. One commentator, however, went further. In an essay called 'I Buy Therefore I Am: the economic meaning of the riots', city broker Dr Tim Morgan says: 'For today's young generation, the message pushed at them by big corporates and the media alike is unmistakable – "you are what you own."' He writes:

The direct promotion of products and services is nothing new, of course, other than in its relentlessly growing scale. The more insidious dimension of the promotion of consumerism lies in its largely successful endeavour to capture lifestyle perceptions. Celebrities, be they sports stars, musicians, actors or the legions of D-list "celebs", are linked to conspicuous consumption. 'You', young people are told, 'ought to live like this.'

The second, flatly contradictory message is that 'you can't have it.' For the average young person, celebrity-style conspicuous consumption is tantalisingly but almost entirely out of reach.

For a young person growing up in a non-rich household, the message, reinforced by peer pressure, is a deeply contradictory blend of 'this is fulfilment' and 'it will forever be out of your reach.' You are, the message says, inadequate if you don't own product X, Y or Z. But you are never going to own them. Compulsive consumerism knows few limits to unattainable aspiration.

It is some measure of the state of panic and of the breakdown of traditional perspectives of left and right that those words, published on 22 August 2011, came from Dr Tim Morgan, global head of research at City of London brokers Tullett Prebon, in a newsletter offering advice to his company's investors. This is what stockbrokers think. If we ever needed Orwell, we need him now.

CHAPTER 1

The Family

As we moved slowly through the outskirts of the town we passed row after row of little grey slum houses running at right angles to the embankment. At the back of one of the houses a young woman was kneeling on the stones, poking a stick up the leaden waste-pipe which ran from the sink inside and which I suppose was blocked. I had time to see everything about her – her sacking apron, her clumsy clogs, her arms reddened by the cold. She looked up as the train passed, and I was almost near enough to catch her eye. She had a round pale face, the usual exhausted face of the slum girl who is twenty-five and looks forty, thanks to miscarriages and drudgery; and it wore, for the second in which I saw it, the most desolate, hopeless expression I have ever-seen. It struck me then that we are mistaken when we say that 'It isn't the same for them as it would be for us,' and that people bred in the slums can imagine nothing but the slums. For what I saw in her face was not the ignorant suffering of an animal. She knew well enough what was happening to her – understood as well as I did how dreadful a destiny it was to be kneeling there in the bitter cold, on the slimy stones of a slum backyard, poking a stick up a foul drain-pipe.

George Orwell, *The Road to Wigan Pier*, 1936

The two men who took nineteen-year-old Sarah D. from her homeless hostel off into the night must have known that she was pregnant. That means they may have been telling the truth when they told her she was going to a large, safe, warm house where there were showers, beds, hot food and a television. There are good Samaritans out there keen to help the distressed and abandoned; hopefully that's who found her. Hopefully two men who take a pretty nineteen-year-old homeless girl back to their house have only her welfare at heart.

If not, if they had a darker intent, then it's hard to know exactly who to blame. Sarah's abusive grandfather and struggling mother have to bear some responsibility, as do the relatives who ignored her – or worse, robbed her blind. But specifically, the reason she was so vulnerable at that particular moment to the offer of comfort, shelter and food is down to a clear chain of failure and betrayal.

I met Sarah at the Pankhurst Centre in Nelson Street, M13 – two Victorian villas sheltering in the glass and concrete arms of Manchester's modern Royal Infirmary – one month before her nineteenth birthday. One of the villas, No. 62, was the home of Emmeline Pankhurst, the leader of the votes-for-women campaign at the turn of the twentieth century. It's now a women's community centre and museum, which runs a weekly drop-in where women can meet up, get a cheap lunch and attend classes and workshops.

Most of the women I met were desperately poor, on benefits and often struggling with mental health issues. One woman's face looked grey with exhaustion – her partner was schizophrenic and had problems sleeping. He would crash out late at night and then wake at odd times, shake her out of her bed and demand she get up. If she managed to spend a few hours at her sister's house, he would call and beg her to come back right away, crying that he needed her. She'd been fighting her own depression, possibly as a result.

Sarah, on the other hand, breezed into the room with a cheerful, open face that rarely stopped smiling, long auburn hair and the confidence of youth. She wondered why we were sitting in the musty old Pankhurst Parlour, a room decked out in its original

Victorian finery, filled with old books and low armchairs. It's because it's the only part of the centre in which men are allowed, I explained. She wrinkled her nose and pronounced this sexist – 'I know it's a women's refuge, but we should have men's refuges as well.'

She liked the drop-in centre but said, in a theatrical whisper, that she found it a bit boring sometimes. 'They give you a lot of help and support with food and getting to places like appointments,' she explained. 'It's just a place apart. They've got the gardening course started now and that's pretty cool to come and do something when you're bored sometimes. It just depends really what you want to come here and do. They've just made bracelets as well and stuff like that – I think we're making T-shirts at two o'clock.'

I wondered if she was a volunteer. No, she was staying just over the road at the Direct Access hostel for homeless women, she replied with a smile. 'I used to live with my mum but I moved out when I was fourteen and then I went into care when I was fifteen,' she said, almost casually. 'I was in care up until I was seventeen turned eighteen, and went to my auntie's for a bit, then I moved to the hostel so I've been pretty much on the road lately.'

And then she told her story – in the same careful, straightforward manner. She described terrible things in a matter-of-fact voice, as if she was discussing a bad day at the office or the script of a TV drama she'd seen the night before – although if that script had a woman recounting her abuse, the writer would have forced tears from the actress's eyes. Sarah, on the other hand, just twisted her mouth in a slightly wry grimace and carried on with her tale.

She was sexually assaulted and repeatedly raped by her grandfather – her mother's father – from the age of twelve. He burdened her with his conspiracy of silence and when the truth finally came out – after three years of abuse – her mum was so torn by the balance of loyalties between her father and her daughter that she struggled to provide the comfort Sarah desperately needed.

'My mum thinks that I blame it on her, which I don't.' She spread her hands out in front of her. 'We have a really weird relationship. It's more of a best friend relationship than a mother and daughter relationship. We just constantly argue. I've got five brothers, all younger than me, and they're all mother's "little boys". I'm more of a daddy's girl but at the minute my dad's in prison so there's not much I can do about it. Preston Prison. It's quite far away so I can only see him like once in a blue moon. So it gets a bit hard for me 'cause I've always turned to my dad rather than my mum. It's like – "oh, I want my daddy . . ."'

She received victim's compensation for the abuse, which seemed welcome until she moved into her auntie's place. 'She borrowed some money off me,' Sarah said, shrugging. 'I did it all legit and the benefits people signed the piece of paper. Gladly enough I'd done it that way because three weeks' after I borrowed my auntie the money she kicked me out. Basically my cousin – she's got a problem with wetting the bed 'cause she's so big. She can't get up at night time. My auntie made me change her bed every time and I got quite sick of changing it. Eventually I said no and it went from there. I got kicked out. So I was happy that I know someone signed it with me and she will have to pay it back. I did have quite a lot of problems with my family. I don't know why . . . families are supposed to be there to love you, really.' She gave a short laugh. 'That's what they're there for.'

Sarah was pregnant when we met. She met her boyfriend at college. He was a chef, working at a curry house on Stockport Road. He was going to stick by her, he said, but was living with his parents and they weren't happy with her moving in.

And so she moved into the hostel – about six weeks before we met. They gave her a room with a sink, a bed and a wardrobe. The washrooms were stacked with dirty clothes and the shower rooms – one to each floor – were streaked with dirt and dotted with broken fixtures. Sometimes there were needles in the showers. Some people were sleeping on chairs. There wasn't anywhere to cook – students came with hot food on Monday, Tuesday and Saturday. On the other days, the only hot option was a takeaway, with its price mark-up and trans-fats and reprocessed meat.

'When I first went in my face was completely clear and now I'm getting loads of spots, which I suppose means I don't like it,' she said, grimacing. 'You've got old women in there, young women, pregnant women – all types of different women. Some of them are alcoholics. Some of them are addicted to heroin and stuff like that. It's dead stressing really 'cause you'll wake up in the morning and you'll think – oh, who's that new face?'

She was hoping, by the end of the month, to move to Birmingham, to another hostel which had a mother and baby unit. 'In Manchester I'm a low priority. If you move to a different area there's a higher chance of you getting on to the housing list. It's supposed to speed the process up quicker or something, I don't know. It just helps.'

Until then she said she was being dead lazy, just eating and sleeping. She had her twelve-week scan coming up – a stage she'd never reached before. She'd always miscarried. Making it to the scan – she was so excited. 'I mean it was dead hard going through miscarriage and then my old relationship with that boyfriend ending and getting kicked out . . . It was dead overwhelming. It weren't just one thing happening, it was fifty million things happening at the same time. The way I've had to look at it is – look, it's happened.

I've got to stop dwelling on the past and think of my future now 'cause it's not only my future I've got to think about now. Touch wood. Hopefully everything will go all right.'

'I go for my first scan at twelve weeks but I missed a week because I was supposed to go for it last week,' she said, giggling awkwardly. 'I didn't end up going for it 'cause I was in bed and missed it but sleep's more important than a scan, isn't it? So I've had to rebook it for next week. But I'll have my next one within three weeks after that and then they do the heartbeat and also . . . Actually, I don't know. I've never got this far before. I think it's quite scary actually. I'm quite nervous about it but I think me nana's going to go with me so I should be all right. Just the thought of that jelly on your belly as well.' And she shivered. 'Dead nervous though. I am still young. Young to be a mum anyway, but you've got to get through that, haven't you?'

She said she had to go and suddenly leaned forward to look over the top of my notebook, catching a glimpse of a list of names.

'Is my name the first name on there?' she grinned.

'No. No, in fact, it isn't unless you're called Amanda . . .'

She smiled and stood up carefully. 'No,' she said. 'My name's Sarah . . .'

I wished her luck with her scan and said I hoped I'd meet her again soon. I told her that I was coming by in a few weeks time and would like to hear how the scan went. 'I should be in Birmingham in the next couple of weeks,' she said with a shrug. 'Fingers crossed.'

And she left. I crossed my fingers – almost a superstition. I didn't cross them hard enough though. I failed her, just like everybody always had. But it took me a while to realize how badly.

Admittedly she had made one mistake – she felt so sleepy, she missed her first scan. Pregnant women do feel sleepy and sick in the first few months, it's not unusual, but Sarah couldn't afford that luxury. She was on benefits in England. As a result of missing the scan, she had no proof she was pregnant. Without that proof, it was easy for the Job Centre to penalize her for turning up late to an interview – sanctioning her off benefits, cutting her money to way below subsistence level. She was an easy target.

Being sanctioned off Jobseeker's Allowance – something only possible since April 2010 – meant her benefits were stopped. No money. She then had to apply for hardship payments, just £28 per week – or £4 per day. Sarah paid £10 per week to the Direct Access hostel, meaning she had £18 a week to live on, or £2.50 per day to feed herself and her growing baby.

'She left the hostel, moved in with an older man, someone she just met, because she had no money,' Caroline, one of the other women at the Pankhurst Centre, told me. 'In the end she thought – let him look after me. They kept stopping her claim and gave her £28 for two weeks. So this older man – who we know is not good for her, she's so vulnerable – he told her he'd got another house, a four-bedroomed house, where she would have a telly, access to a cooker, heating, food . . . What would you do? What choice did she have? I went over to see her but she'd left the night before. We haven't managed to speak to her since.'

The grim truth is that Sarah probably had her benefit money taken away to meet an internal target created for political advantage and, as a result, was forced into who knows what. Since the Labour government introduced benefit sanctions in April 2000, around 20,000 people per month have had benefits withdrawn, usually for a few weeks, sometimes for months. The number started to rise in the summer of 2010. In March 2011, more than 43,000 people had benefits taken away as some form of punishment for anything from filling out a form wrongly, turning up late to an interview or fraudulent claims.

In April 2011, the *Guardian* spoke to a whistleblower who claimed that staff at his Job Centre were given targets of three people a week to refer for sanctions. He said it was part of a 'culture change' since last summer that had led to competition between advisers, teams and regional offices.

'Suddenly you're not helping somebody into sustainable employment, which is what you're employed to do,' he told journalist John Domokos. 'You're looking for ways to trick your customers into "not looking for work". You come up with many ways. I've seen dyslexic customers given written job searches, and when they don't produce them – what a surprise – they're sanctioned. The only target that anyone seems to care about is stopping people's money.'

The Department of Work and Pensions protested vigorously at the very idea of this. Then it checked and admitted that, yes, perhaps that had been the case but it would now ask everyone to stop. In April, the month Sarah was sanctioned, more than 31,000 people had some form of benefit withdrawn as a punishment or fine. Since April 2000, there have been almost four million handed out.

The idea comes from research in the United States that seems to suggest that sanctions 'strongly reduce benefit use and raise exits from benefits'. The same research, however, shows sanctions have a terrible effect on earnings over time, child well-being, job quality and crime rates. You can beat people into work with threats and fines, but you get unhappy people doing unsuitable jobs, with crime on the rise and children suffering. You also get young, abused girls vanishing from the streets.

A few days after my conversation with Caroline, filled with guilt, I tried to report Sarah missing to the police. I wasn't a friend, I wasn't a relative, I was just a journalist worried about a homeless girl and I couldn't

prove I knew her surname or that she was pregnant. The
woman on the phone sounded dubious at best but said
I shouldn't worry. Hopefully she's fine. It just doesn't
do to be poor at the moment.

When Orwell set out on *The Road to Wigan Pier*, it was
also a very bad time to be poor. The Depression was in
its sixth year, the coalition government was revamping
unemployment benefit and introducing intrusive tests
to be sure people qualified. Groups such as the
Unemployed Workers' Movement organized marches
and protests, using tactics similar to recent student
protests over tuition fees or the Occupy protest outside
St Paul's Cathedral.

Orwell arrived in Wigan on a Saturday morning early
in February. He walked from Wigan station to the
home of a local activist, Gerry Kennan, on the Beech
Hill council estate. Kennan found him lodgings that
were too respectable for Orwell's taste – he wanted to
see things 'at their worst' so followed his tramp's nose
to the common lodging house and tripe shop at 22
Darlington Street, where the book opens, with its slab
'upon which lay the great white folds of tripe, and the
grey flocculent stuff known as "black tripe", and the
ghostly translucent feet of pigs, ready boiled'.

Kennan arranged meetings and tours of coal mines,
but Orwell also spent time wandering the streets,
especially the crowded, industrial Scholes district

around Darlington Street. On a long, slow Wednesday afternoon – half-day closing in Wigan in 1936 – he bumped into a gang of kids hanging round on a street corner. One of them, a newspaper boy called Sid Smith, later remembered 'this tall, gangly man wearing Oxford bags who had a tousled appearance and carried a clipboard. He began asking questions such as, "Where do you work? How much do you earn? How long is your working week?" We thought he was a government snooper, trying to catch people out on the Means Test.' The boys kept quiet and Orwell moved on, checking houses inside and out, asking about rents and conditions in the packed terraced houses and the few two-up two-downs remaining. He wrote:

Words are such feeble things. 'What is the use of a brief phrase like 'roof leaks' or 'four beds for eight people'? It is the kind of thing your eye slides over, registering nothing. And yet what a wealth of misery it can cover! Take the question of over-crowding, for instance. Quite often you have eight or even ten people sleeping in two small rooms, probably in at most four beds. In one house, I remember, three grown-up girls shared the same bed and all went to work at different hours, each disturbing the others when she got up or came in; in another house a young miner working on the night shift slept by day in a narrow bed in which another member of the family slept by night. Then there is the misery of leaking roofs and oozing walls, which in winter makes some rooms almost uninhabitable. Then there are bugs. Once bugs get into a house they are in it till the crack of doom; there is no sure way of exterminating them.

Of course, Orwell was wrong. Words are not feeble things. His own words in *Wigan Pier* joined the depictions of misery in Seebohm Rowntree's 1936 survey of poverty and the concrete suggestions in John Maynard Keynes' 1936 book, *The General Theory of Employment, Interest and Money*, in a thundering critique of a failing system. Crystallized in the 1941 Beveridge Report's attack on the five evils of 'Want, Disease, Ignorance, Squalor and Idleness' all these words helped build an ambitious post-war project to make poverty history – a project that was, at one point, deemed so successful that poverty in the UK ceased to exist.

If anything, Orwell's words were too powerful. Many people who I talked to in Wigan dislike the book intensely. There's a feeling that it lumbered the town with a particular reputation – the journalistic equivalent of a Lowry painting, all cloth caps, tripe, whippets and two-up two-down terraced housing with outside toilets. Wigan has become synonymous with Orwell's vivid descriptions of subsistence-level poverty, filthy slums and dirty faces.

The truth is more complicated. Since Orwell actively sought out the worst housing, the darkest industrial landscapes and the most brutal working conditions he could find, the book's early pages describe the clumping of mill-girls' clogs down cobbled Wigan streets, Orwell being forced to share a bed in his lodging house and his breakfasting on a table that conceals a chamber pot brimming full with waste – yet much of northwest England was already moving on. The slums were being cleared as Orwell wrote about them. In 1936 there were extensive garden cities, modern council houses, electric lighting and a flourishing consumer society. Orwell mentions kids in Manchester buying Savile Row suits on hire purchase, football pools and the spread of radio sets.

Indeed, just five years later in his 1941 essay *The Lion and the Unicorn: Socialism and the English Genius*, he reframes the British working class in very modern terms:

> Nearly all citizens . . . now enjoy the use of good roads, germ-free water, police protection, free libraries and probably free education of a kind . . . As to housing, England still has slums which are a blot on civilization, but much building has been done during the past ten years, largely by the local authorities. The modern council house, with its bathroom and electric light, is smaller than the

stockbroker's villa, but it is recognizably the same kind of house, which the farm labourer's cottage is not. A person who has grown up in a council housing estate is likely to be – indeed, visibly *is* – more middle class in outlook than a person who has grown up in a slum.

Orwell could take some small part of the credit for this, but he also fixed the image of British poverty as cobbles, caps and clogs. Whilst writing this book, I was asked a number of times to compare 1936 with today in direct, financial terms in order to prove poverty is as bad now as it was in 1936. The truth is that it's very hard to compare directly, for all the reasons Orwell listed in his 1941 essay.

What does poverty mean today? The debate abounds with vague terms – Absolute Poverty, Relative Poverty, Social Disenfranchisement . . . the nuances of these definitions aren't necessarily obvious but can matter desperately. In the United States over the summer of 2011, for instance, there were suggestions that anyone considered to be living in relative poverty but who owned a refrigerator should face a huge tax increase.

The oldest idea of Absolute Poverty is something you can apply internationally to any society – $2 per day according to the United Nations. Relative Poverty, on the other hand, means families whose income falls below 60 per cent of the national median – the median being the halfway point between the richest and the poorest. If the richest earns £100 per week and the poorest earns £0, the median is £50 and the poverty line is £30. In 2011, that Relative Poverty line comes in at roughly £240 per week – out of which you'll have to pay housing, heating, food, clothes, water, travel, council tax and on and on.

The Institute for Fiscal Studies (IFS) and the Department for Work and Pensions (DWP) have finessed these figures into a chart depending on your circumstances. For a single adult, Relative Poverty means £165 per week, for a couple with a kid that's £256 per week and a couple with two kids aged eight or over are at the poverty line on £346 per week.

In the UK, things are further complicated – the 1997 Labour government used the term Absolute Poverty to describe households with an income less than 50 per cent of the average income in 1997. This definition lasted until the 2011 Child Poverty Act, when the coalition government set a new UK benchmark – any household whose income is below 60 per cent of the 2010–11 UK average weekly wage of £411. In Britain, your Absolute Poverty depends on the year your government was elected and is also, clearly, relative.

According to the DWP statistics, in 2009–10, 29 per cent of children – 3.8 million kids – were living in both relative and absolute poverty as were 7.9 million adults – 22 per cent of the adult population. In Wigan, 12,875 children live in poverty – out of a population of 306,000. According to the IFS, this will get worse. 'The long-term effects of the recession and higher inflation eroding living standards is yet to be felt,' it argued in a report analysing those numbers.

You can sniff at the label and consider it way too generous a definition of poverty – the incomes are a lot higher than $2 per day. But the idea of starvation-level Absolute Poverty hasn't been in serious use in the UK since Seebohm Rowntree, poverty researcher and son of the chocolate-manufacturing philanthropist Joseph, abandoned it in the year Orwell strode the northwest.

Rowntree senior, steered by his Quaker beliefs, founded the Joseph Rowntree Foundation to research poverty using his cocoa-bean fortune. His son was so fascinated by the debate as to what counted as poverty that he published a survey of conditions in York in 1899. Back then the concept of unemployment was new – the word was coined in the 1880s when it became clear that the complete absence of jobs in the once prosperous cotton towns in Lancashire could not be blamed on a few feckless men and women. Fecklessness hardly went in cycles.

Seebohm's 1899 survey was published two years later as *Poverty: A Study of Town Life*. To ensure his measure of the money needed for a subsistence level of existence was accurate, he included fuel, light, rent, food, clothing and household items in his list of essential costs. In 1899, by his measure, 27.8 per cent of the population of York was living in poverty.

His work was considered scandalous for reasons we might recognize today – people rebelled against the argument that poverty was the result of low wages instead of the traditionally held view that the poor were responsible for their own plight.

Revisiting his study in 1936, Rowntree reconsidered what counted as essential. He cut people the same kind of slack as Orwell, who argued that everybody needed a cup of tea, a pint and a cigarette now and then. Second time round, therefore, Seebohm included in his list of essential costs things not strictly necessary for survival. In calculating the minimum money people needed, he argued that newspapers, books, radios, beer, tobacco, holidays and presents were fundamental to a meaningful life. By these criteria, Rowntree estimated that 31.1 per cent of the population of York was living in poverty in 1936. Similarly, 17.3 per cent were living in relative poverty in Merseyside during 1929–30, 20 per cent in Southampton in 1931, and 10.7 per cent in Bristol in 1936.

It's tempting to compare those numbers with DWP data showing 54 per cent of children in Scholes are today living in poverty, and to conclude that things are absolutely worse, but it's hard to make an accurate comparison. Poverty has to be relative, just as the imperative for you, as a child, to clean your plate was relative to your time – things have changed. If a low-income family struggles with debt, can't afford to pay the bills this winter and sees it's loved ones die young it doesn't help to say that the poor in 1936 didn't have electricity or bank accounts. Nor does it help to say 'at least you're not starving in Africa'. We don't live in 1936 or Africa. Our needs are different.

During the last decade, the poorest one-tenth of the population have seen, on average, a fall in income after paying housing costs whilst the richest have seen their income soar. If you're poor, you're unhappy. If you're poor whilst everyone else is getting richer, you're angry. Orwell knew this. He counted out pay packets for employed and unemployed – one miner took home less than £2 per week (worth between £100 and £380 per week today depending on your currency converter) whilst one unemployed couple lived on thirty-two shillings a week (between £80 and £300 per week by the same measures). Despite his experiences in Burma and down and out in Paris and London, Orwell knew this was too little.

'An Englishman on the P.A.C. (Public Assistance Committee – which set and distributed unemployment benefit) gets fifteen shillings a week because fifteen shillings is the smallest sum on which he can conceivably keep alive,' Orwell wrote. 'If he were, say, an Indian or Japanese coolie, who can live on rice and onions, he wouldn't get fifteen shillings a week – he would be lucky if he got fifteen shillings a month.' Fifteen shillings a week in England would seem a fortune elsewhere but Orwell was amazed by the privations people suffered to get by on so little in the UK.

Today, the same is true. To feel what poverty is like, spend time with Micky, who lives in Ashton, to the east of Manchester. He's long-term unemployed and trying to get into work but has a host of instant support packages – council tax benefit, things to do with child maintenance, all sorts of bits and pieces going on. He's got a daughter, but he no longer lives with her mother so he's got responsibilities but he lives alone. He's not lazy. He works as a volunteer for Social Enterprise doing fire safety checks in homes. In some ways he's working so hard he doesn't have time for a job. He and his team inspect very poor houses on very rough estates, looking at all private properties and trying to prevent them from bursting into flames.

Fire and poverty aren't directly linked in the way they were when houses were built of wood and straw but it's true that the poorer you are the more likely you are to start a fire. This shouldn't be true but it is. It's often to do with trying to squeeze everything you can out of the smallest things, with no one saying things like 'sensibly you can't put that many plugs in that socket'. Or stuff you might not know, like how to get a free smoke alarm, for example.

In 1947, fire brigades first gained the duty to do public health checks in order to reduce fires as well as putting them out. They were given a greater role in various Fire Safety Acts in 1971 and 1997, and finally – in 2004 – the Fire Rescue and Services Act section 6 specified that a fire and rescue authority must make provision for the purpose of promoting fire safety in its area by a proactive strategy targeted at all sections of the community.

As they started going into houses they saw the reasons for the fire hazards such as big extension leads covered in plugs or people trying to heat one room in the cheapest way possible – on a one bar heater. 'It's actually not going to be that safe a heater,' Micky explained. 'It's probably not going to be that new so it's not going to be very efficient either.' People would also sit so close to their single oil-fired radiator, with flammable blankets all around them, that it would create further risk of fire.

In terms of alleviating housing inequalities, the house visits are one of the things that really work – because no one minds the fire service coming to call. When a policeman comes to your door, you are usually wary, but when the fire or ambulance service come people are generally friendly. This isn't always the case, of course, so in places like Ashton and Ince, Greater Manchester, the fire service has a Community Action Team who wear a subtler version of the uniform, a polo shirt and a fleece: they still look professional but they're not in shiny fire suits.

For people who fear they're going to lose their children when anyone in authority knocks on the door, having a volunteer who you know, who lives just down the road, makes a difference. And Micky makes a difference. He visits houses, does fire checks and directs people to local services, and he absolutely loves doing it. But he doesn't get paid for it.

He's on disability benefit so he's very careful with his money – he would like to have enough to spend on his daughter, to buy her things she wants. He doesn't want her dreading a visit to her dad, thinking her mum's the nice parent and way more generous. Micky doesn't like to think this way, because he and his ex get along and he knows his daughter would never think that really, but he just wants to provide for her like a dad should. So he tries to ration his weekly money – for instance, he's careful how he eats He'll make curry or chilli with a 15p tin of mince and a 12p tin of tomatoes and some premixed sauce or spices. The cheapest mince is in the superstore but the cheapest chilli mix is in a corner shop almost a mile away. So he walks between the two shops to buy his food and he gets enough to last for six days. He's found different ways to eat it, because he can't afford to pay the fuel cost to heat rice every day – which would be the nice thing to eat in the traditional 'let's make it a nice dinner' fashion. Instead, he has curried mince on toast some days and cold chilli sandwiches another day, but on Sunday he'll find enough for a meal for when his daughter comes over.

Micky, by some people's yardstick, is evil scrounging scum. He is a council tax cheat for one thing. Not voluntarily, but by default. He lives on his own and gets a single-person discount on council tax. The council pays his council tax benefit, but somehow they overpay about £30 a month in council tax benefit, which they then claim back from him a couple of times a year.

He's trying to survive on a 12p tin of mince even though he gets an extra £30 a month, but he knows that someone's going to ask for it back. It may be his daughter's birthday that month but he's too scared to dip into that £30 because he knows at some point it will have to be returned, and if he can't pay then he could wind up homeless or, as has happened to people in Northampton, Manchester, Bristol, Liverpool, Doncaster and countless other towns and cities across the UK over the past couple of years, in jail.

He's written to the council, saying: 'I don't want the money, don't give it to me, I can manage, why can't you just pay me the council tax that you charge me? You're administering both systems . . .' But he lives in that world where arguing with people gets you nowhere at all. Nobody listens to a word you say. You're that shouty man who says 'your system is insane, what are you doing?'

Micky is helping to prevent houses from burning down and helping to keep the people who live in them alive. He's doing a public service that's financially supported by the council. And yet the council – through no fault of Micky's – puts his home and freedom at risk thanks to an administrative error. This system clearly needs to exist but there's a lack of sense within it –it just doesn't work.

Micky is an articulate man. He thinks most people are rational. He knows that when you explain his predicament too anyone will see it's irrational. But no one seems to be able to change it. Micky says the strange thing is that he never thought that one aspect of being powerless would be not being able to say I don't want this money . . .

Mickey is one of ten million Britons who earn less than £15,000 a year – the basic amount, according to the Joseph Rowntree Foundation, that an individual needs to earn to reach a minimum socially acceptable standard of living. He's in Relative Poverty. What's shocking is how much better off he is than at least twenty people I met in cities across the northwest of England who were living close to United Nations-style Absolute Poverty.

Sarah D.'s tragedy isn't just that she only had £2.50 a day to feed herself and her newborn baby after her benefits were cut off, it's that her case is not that exceptional.

*

Poverty isn't just about money, as Orwell knew. The housing conditions that Orwell felt words could notdescribe are everywhere. In Scholes, just down the road from Orwell's former lodging house, there's a family of asylum seekers – mum, dad and three boys – who lived in a house for five years on funding from an asylum-seekers charity. They were all doing well in education, integrated even by the exacting standards of the local residents association and active in the local community. However, when the eldest boy hit eighteen, the funding dried up and they were made homeless. They ended up in a two-room flat with no kitchen, with all five of them sleeping in one room. Six months later they were still there.

In nearby Springfield, Simon, twenty-six, rents a flat for £400 per month, consisting of a broken armchair with rusted metal springs popping out, loose light fittings, dry rot, damp stains on the wall, broken taps, kitchen cabinet doors hanging off, an open pipe leading to the drains, windows sealed with masking tape, and earwigs and slugs creeping around.

'I feel like I'm being robbed blind but have no alternative,' he explains. 'I rang the Environmental Health but the landlord told me if I carried on with them I could be evicted. I can smell the damp whilst taking a bath, I wake up cold and I can see my own breath when I visit the toilet. If the monthly bills get too high, the landlord switches off the electricity at

11.30 p.m. I would love to move somewhere else where I am in charge of my own electricity bill, where I am not manipulated to what I can and can't have, but I can't raise the deposit and advance rent payment.'

How can this be? Of course, the first tragedy of this question is that anyone should ask it. Rowntree's third round of poverty research in 1950 concluded that neither Absolute nor Relative Poverty existed in the UK – the welfare state had entirely eradicated the problem. Poverty was history.

The second tragedy is how we threw that away. Take the people Orwell met in Wigan, for instance. Gerry Kennan stayed in the union movement, his son Harry worked in the merchant navy, then as an electrician in the mines and then moved to Heinz when the company opened a factory nearby. Harry fought for, and won, union recognition at the plant. He retired, grew carnations and doted on his wife and daughters – still living on Beech Hill Estate, in a modern semi-detached house with a view across the whole town. He died in October 2011.

After the Second World War, Sid Smith's magazine stand grew and grew until it took up most of one side of a Wigan arcade, with a huge banner bearing the proud 'This Is Smiths' flapping above. In the 1970s, he added books and music at the behest of his son Trevor – who joined the family business after a brief teaching career – and they relocated to a shop nearby. In the

1980s, by then one of the largest independent retailers in Wigan, father and son snapped up a local bakery to give them a sprawling 10,000-foot store. When Trevor finally sold up in 2006 – his two daughters had little interest in the family business – Smiths employed twenty-eight staff and boasted 30,000 books on its extensive shelves.

Trevor Smith now lives in Wrightington – a village at the edge of Wigan Borough. His house stands at the end of a winding country lane and from his windows the views stretch out over rolling green hills. Hanging on the walls are silver discs signed by the Spice Girls and Take That – gratitude for helping sales top one million each. The newsagent game proved lucrative indeed.

Trevor sold up at the right time – he suffered a massive heart attack shortly afterwards, for one thing, and his successor struggled to make a go of it in the new world of online competition. The shop closed in 2009. 'People didn't think folk in Wigan would buy books,' Trevor recalls. 'They were wrong. But I think people expect Coronation Street. Yes, it was bad. It's not so bad now.'

Jim Hammond, who could have been the poster boy for hard-working poverty, showed Orwell around some of the Wigan pits. Hammond had left school at fourteen and went straight down the mines. He would lie on his back chipping coal from a seam inches away from his face and was paid per bucket. By 1936 he was out of work – banned from the pits for organizing strikes. His wife was six months pregnant with their son Tony when she met Orwell.

Tony Hammond is the perfect post-war British version of the American dream. Born in Park Hospital, Davyhulme – where Nye Bevan launched the National Health Service – he grew up sleeping three to a room, living in houses without running water and using outdoor toilets designed for municipal carts to carry off the sewage. He recieved free school meals during the war, then came a scholarship to Wigan Grammar School, followed by law at Oxford and called to the bar . . . in one generation everything changed.

His children Maggie and Katie qualified as solicitors whilst Fanny works as a teacher in Northern Ireland. His grandchildren are all doing well – Jamie is reading medicine, Tom is reading politics, Jessica has just completed a year in Germany on an Erasmus scholarship, Emily wants to do nursing at Queens, and the youngest, Olivia, plays netball for Northern Ireland and is heading for Oxford.

Tony retired as a judge three years ago and now lives in Didsbury, Manchester. We met in his tennis club, sipping Belgian lager and waiting for his quiz team to assemble. He remembers his grandparent's house in Lowe Street clearly – Orwellian in the Wigan sense. The front door opened into the living room. The floor was stone-flagged and covered with rugs. There was a big

Yorkshire range filling the kitchen where his grandmother, literally until the moment she died, used to sit on a stool, leaning against the range, doing her knitting.

During the Second World War, he explains, his dad managed to get work in the pits again – there was a war on, they needed miners. He was a union organizer within two years. It can't have paid badly – Tony remembers being the only house in the street with a telly at the time of Elizabeth II's coronation.

Tony is a powerfully built man, with a stern judge's face that he can bring out when discussing the finer points of coal-mining history. The only time his commanding presence falters is when discussing his dad.

At one point, discussing how hard his father fought over pit props and how wages were ratcheted up through canny schemes to get details of the price of coal early, he detours to talk about the work his dad had to do between the wars, when he was banned from the pits for being a communist. He took any job, all sorts, even working as a seaman on a leaky oil tanker called the *Scottish Musician* . . . he saw him drunk only once, when he'd won cheap coal for the Wigan miners and the man from the Coal Board had to carry him home. And then Tony stops, and says how proud he is of his father, and his eyes fill with tears. 'It's quite a story, isn't it?' he almost whispers.

It could seem as if Orwell's touch sprinkled some kind of magic over the lives of those he met. In reality, of course, he was wandering fairly aimlessly through working-class areas in the northwest. Sid Smith, Gerry Kennan and Jim Hammond weren't quite chance meetings – Gerry and Jim were self-selected by virtue of their active trade union membership – but they were as close to an average sampling of the Scholes district as any opinion pollster would find. That their children achieved so much was partly down to education, partly down to the welfare state, partly down to class mobility and partly down to the dreams they held and realized.

Sid Smith was the first person to persuade the Football Association to sell FA Cup programmes in newsagents across the country and not just at Wembley Stadium. Gerry Kennan's son Harry was so determined to look after his workmates that Wigan's Heinz plant has the best health and safety and shift-payment system in Europe. Jim Hammond's son – the unemployable communist miner's son – became an Oxbridge-educated judge. Could anyone, apart from a politician campaigning for election, believe that kids in Scholes in 2011 have any chance of such a future?

I met a twelve-year-old kid in a community centre in Scholes whose dad drank himself to death and whose mum is heading the same way. He's on free school meals, can't go on school trips unless a local charity pays – the same charity that sometimes has to pay for his shoes and his school uniform – and he's never been outside Wigan. His mum gets £108 per week, he says. 'She has to put £35 on gas and £35 on electric. That lasts one week.' Some days, when there's no food, he lives on a bowl of cereal. If he's at school, he gets dinner. If not, that's his lot. He thinks about being a vet because there are men on his estate who breed and sell dogs. For that to happen, for him to become a vet, he believes a magician will have to come and cast a spell.

Eileen is fifty-four years old and used to live in Little Horton, Bradford. She's so ill and tired she hunches forward when talking, letting the folds of her cardigan and her crossed forearms cover her body. Her elbows rest on her knees and her hands knit nervously by her face, the stance of a long-term smoker.

Earlier this year, she'd fallen so far behind on various debts – rent, bills, council tax, TV licence – that she had to move out of her council house. 'The house was all right,' she says, without a trace of bitterness. 'It was a three-bedroom house. I'd got lovely neighbours – I'd got Asian neighbours on one side, Asian neighbours on the other and the Asian lady who lived at number 58, she still comes to see me. She phones me and asks me where I am and she'll come up and see me. I got on with everybody. Everybody called me Aunty Eileen, even the Asian boys, Mr Shah's kids. I've watched all them grow up. The oldest one's about twenty-nine now, married and got children and he still calls me

Aunty Eileen. I do get on with everybody, you know, it's just so hard . . . you haven't got the money, you can't do anything.'

It's not like hard times are new to Eileen. When she was growing up, her four brothers, mother and stepfather all lived in a one-bedroom cottage that became so crowded she moved out to live with her granddad – her stepfather's father.

'I was ten and it was the time I had ladies things.' She blushes a little, her careworn face flushing a light pink. 'I wasn't happy because I was a tomboy and when I lived there we used to go out scrapping – you know, picking scrap lead up with my brothers. We used to get all we could, rummage round the dump then my dad would weigh it and sell it. They still do it now. I know kids still go out young as nine and ten, "have you got any old scrap?" and they're waiting, their dads' waiting. The dealers are out West Bowling – still Bradford 5, Bradford 4, all along the Manchester Road.'

What is new to Eileen is the pain of loss. She's worked all her life – at Netto and at the local bingo hall, where she rose to manageress before the death of her son Jamie, aged thirty-two. 'I had five children, I lost Jamie four years this December, and when I lost him I just went downhill. I were working and I were poorly and I went back to work poorly. When I went back I couldn't really manage so I weren't getting enough wages to cover everything. I were working, I had to pay

full rent and because I had my daughters there –
because both of them lived with me at the time – I
didn't get nowt knocked off, I still had to pay full rent.
They had to help towards things but they were
unemployed. I'd leave one bill one time and then I'd
leave another one the next time and then that's – that's
why I lost my home. I owe nearly £2,000 in rent.'

Eileen can stay at her daughter's house for a few
nights – although she has osteoporosis and finds
sleeping on the sofa painful. Because she's trying to pay
back her debts, especially the TV licence people who are
threatening her with prison – 'I don't think I could cope
in prison', Eileen says – she gets £111 a fortnight, or
just under £8 per day. She gives her daughter
something if she stops there for a couple of days, to
help with the gas and electric.

And she's got a dog, which sucks at her cash. She
found her in Morecambe – a three-month old puppy
owned by a nightclub bouncer who used to put out
cigarettes on the dog's back as punishment for making
a mess in his flat. 'You leave a puppy and it will chew,
it will mess, it will wee and he didn't like that because
he wasn't going home till four,' Eileen says, with more
indignation than she showed for her own plight. 'I
found out and I paid £30 for her and I've had her ever
since.'

The dog always eats well; Eileen less so. The day
before we met she'd had cups of tea with sugar, some

biscuits and a pear. It was three in the afternoon when we spoke and she hadn't eaten anything that day. 'I am hungry, I'm really hungry but I can do without, if I have a cup of tea then I'm sound and I do like my cups of tea – not coffee, tea. If I've got a cup of tea I'm fine.'

She tries to avoid staying with her son in case he takes some of what little cash she's got. She doesn't really get on with him. She knows it sounds horrible, but he's on methadone. He went down that road after her other son died. She's not sure if it's because he lost his brother but she got him help and she got him on to methadone but he likes to smoke weed and if she can't give him money he kicks off and calls her all sorts. She tries to keep away and see him only when he comes to his sister's. Her youngest daughter is nineteen and the next one's twenty-two. The twenty-two year-old has turned to alcohol. She jumped out of a window the Tuesday before we met – she broke her back and now she's at home with a brace on. The nineteen-year-old has never had employment. She's applied for cleaning jobs but she hasn't got them because she's too young or she's inexperienced.

At one point, while we were talking, Eileen started to cry. It was all the more alarming because she spoke so calmly about so many terrible things. 'We've lived, we've worked, we've got nothing,' she began, then the tears came. 'It's horrible, there's nowt to look forward to, there's nowt to fetch kids into this world. I've worked all my life and I've got nothing to show. I get my clothes from the second-hand shops because I can't afford to buy new. It hasn't got any better, it's got worse in fact. The riots haven't started just because somebody's got killed, it's because it needed to be done this, because nobody's getting a word in. Nobody's getting a word in and this is their way of expressing themselves which is wrong but it's – there's no future, there is no future.'

It's hard to convey the emotion, the pain of this woman who had lost her son, who now slept on her daughter's sofa with her back causing her terrible pain. The list of her troubles is so long, it's hard to get a perspectiove on them and it's easy to see it as a litany of misery. It's easy to lose sight of the person amidst the pain.

Eileen could just be a cipher, a lost soul, a vanishing point – but her life came briefly into view as Andrea Dunbar's best friend. Dunbar was the Bradford-born teenage playwright who wrote *Rita, Sue and Bob Too*, which became Alan Clarke's 1987 film about two Bradford teenagers who have a fling with a married man. The script was autobiographical – Sue was based on Andrea, Rita had some crossover with Eileen. So for a few years Eileen was nearly famous.

In the second half of the film, Sue moves in with an Asian taxi driver but flees with Rita when he becomes too controlling. In real life it was Eileen that Andrea escaped with after Yussuf began to beat her. Eileen sneaked Andrea and her daughter Lorraine out of the bedroom window, picked up her eldest, Jamie, and they fled to Keighley. 'Not for long,' Eileen says, her face lit up at the memory of her friend. 'We got found. We was old enough to run away – I was twenty-two. So we went back, lived next door to each other on the Arbor. She watched my kids grow up.' Long pause. 'And then, you know, she died at twenty-nine. From that brain haemorrhage.'

In 2010, Clio Barnard directed a film about Dunbar's life – called *The Arbor* after one of her plays. It told Dunbar's story: born in 1961 on the Buttershaw Estate, she was fifteen when she wrote *The Arbor* for a school CSE project, but eighteen when she submitted it to the Royal Court Young Writers' Festival. The play was staged at the Royal Court in 1980, directed by Max Stafford-Clark, and Dunbar was hailed as a powerful working-class voice. Shelagh Delaney – herself a working-class teenager when her play *A Taste of Honey* made her famous in 1958 – called Dunbar 'a genius straight from the slums with black teeth and a brilliant smile'.

After merging *The Arbor* with the stage play of *Rita, Sue and Bob Too* to make the movie script, Dunbar achieved some tabloid fame. She had an *Arena* documentary devoted to her and was pursued by the press. She dismissed the attention, saying; 'There's people in Buttershaw a lot more clever than I could ever be. I just stumbled across this writing by accident, whereas other people haven't had the opportunity to get out and do that.'

Andrea stayed and died on the estate – drinking heavily in her local pub, the Beacon, until the night she died in 1990. At the end of chapter one in *The Road to Wigan Pier*, Orwell leaves the town through slag-heaps, chimneys, piled scrap-iron, foul canals, paths of cindery mud criss-crossed by the prints of clogs. Leaving Bradford today, you pass derelict factories and mills lining the railway track, their windows smashed and chimneys still.

Whilst leaving Wigan Orwell saw that girl from the window of his train – the young woman kneeling on the stones. He had time to see everything about her – her exhausted face with the most desolate, hopeless expression he had ever seen. He realized there was no difference between people – that we are all just the same, and there but for the grace of God . . .

Leaving Bradford, I read old newspaper clippings about Andrea and her daughter Lorraine; half-Asian on an all-white estate, raped at fourteen, exposed early to crack and heroin, she endured prostitution and domestic violence, and was imprisoned for involvement in a robbery. In 2006, Lorraine's one-year-old son Harris died after taking some of his mother's methadone. Lorraine, called Samaya Rafiq after converting to Islam, was convicted of his manslaughter.

'They'll forget all about us by tomorrow,' Andrea predicted in a 1980s interview. She was almost right.

CHAPTER 2

Work

Our civilization, pace Chesterton, is founded on coal, more completely than one realizes until one stops to think about it. The machines that keep us alive, and the machines that make machines, are all directly or indirectly dependent upon coal. In the metabolism of the Western world the coal-miner is second in importance only to the man who ploughs the soil. He is a sort of caryatid upon whose shoulders nearly everything that is not grimy is supported.

George Orwell, *The Road to Wigan Pier*, 1936

'Mining was the thing that really interested him,' explains Professor Stephen Ingle, author of *The Social and Political Thought of George Orwell*. He continues:

When he got the commission to go to the north, what he saw his task as being was to elicit the sympathy of the general readership for people on the rack. What he actually found were people with resilience, values, culture and something that he called socialism. What I think he meant by socialism is a kind of Christian support and value system alongside a sense of solidarity and a strong work ethic. I think he was rather in awe of some of the people he met.

In chapter two, Orwell visited a coal mine in Wigan – it almost killed him: 'Most of the things one imagines in hell are there – heat, noise, confusion, darkness, foul air, and, above all, unbearably cramped space,' he wrote. He envied the miners' toughness and doubted the virtue of his own effete intellectualism.

Seventy-five years on, life down a mine has changed but much has also remained the same. Machines do much of the brute digging work, but for those amongst the 5,000 miners left in the UK who work a coalface it's still tough, brutal and dangerous. Mick Trueman is a supervisor at Maltby pit near Rotherham. He's a huge bear of a man, friendly and even a little awkward although his nickname in the pit is 'lash' because he whips the men into line.

'Mining's medieval really,' he explains. 'We haven't got mobile phones and the internet down there. It's mining, it's hard toil, it's dust. I've been supervisor for fourteen years. At the other pit, I was on the air pit. I was setting steel arches. Shovelling all day. When I come out I'm covered in dust, so thick you wouldn't recognize me. What's on the face is fine because you can wash it off, but that's in the lungs as well, every day. There are times when I get up and I'm coughing up the black – it just gets worse.'

Trueman gets up at 4.45 a.m., has a cup of tea and gets to work to find out what they've done on the other shifts. He pulls his team together and locks into the lift, heading down 1,000 metres, then, once underground, travelling five miles out to the coalface. They have a conveyor from the pit bottom that takes him the first two or three miles and then the men get out and walk the rest.

At the coalface its 44°F. Everyone is dripping with sweat. Mick's had an ear infection for five years. A doctor has told him his eardrum is inverted. Infection gets in, there's sweat in his ears all day long – it's perfect for breeding. They cauterized his ear and told him to stop getting it wet. They advised him to come out of the pit.

'I'm not the smartest kid on the block,' he shrugs. 'I struggled at school, I was a bit dyslexic but I was born 200 metres from the mine. Basically, in them days – when you're fifteen you go to the mine. Your dad were there. If your dad had a job you were guaranteed a job. It were a family thing. I've tried to get out a few times and better myself, but it's never worked out. So I've gone back. The money's double what else you can get. But in the last ten years you want to be looking elsewhere otherwise it's going to get you. It's the hazards. I've seen injuries. One guy, a lump came off the roof, 10 ft by 4 ft – it took his arm off. We're allowed to give morphine because they can't get to them quick enough. As you get older you realize that you've just got to hope it's not you. We try and win the lottery – we do it every week. I've done thirty years so I should be used to it but I'd like to think for that last fifteen years of my life I could do something I really like.'

Trueman hopes for something different for his two sons Jamie and Bradley. In an area of high long-term unemployment, however, Maltby pit is still the biggest employer. In the spring, owners Hargreaves Services added a fifth shift to increase production at the mine – which will now work round the clock. The price of coal and coke is surging, so Maltby's cutting equipment will operate for all but three hours in a week and, in total, seventy new jobs are being created. In Rotherham – where twelve dole claimants chase every vacancy against a national average of six per vacancy – seventy jobs are welcome but just nowhere near enough. In March 2011, there were 7,854 people claiming Jobseeker's Allowance. Seventy jobs isn't even a dent.

Edward Murphy runs Merseyside Network for Change, a voluntary sector organization helping the long-term unemployed find work. He's been involved in creating jobs for years – on Liverpool City Council's Economic Development Committee and heading up the government's New Deal programme in the city. We met in his small office in a disused warehouse near the city centre. 'When Orwell went to the north the situation was one of long-term periods of work broken up by brief periods of unemployment,' he explained. 'Now it's long-term periods of unemployment broken up by government schemes.'

Of course, the pit Orwell clambered down has closed. All the mines around Wigan have closed. In fact, most of the mines in Britain have closed. In 1983 there were 170 coal mines. Now there are four. There are various reasons – Britain became more reliant on oil, old labour-heavy mines were no longer economic, energy policy changed, some mines literally ran out of coal . . . but there's also a political reason. Successive governments have had plans for the mines and the miners from the beginning of the Industrial Revolution onwards – usually involving large-scale social engineering.

From the 1950s and 1960s, there are Hansard debates and secret documents in the Cabinet archive discussing the closure of pit towns and the coalfields – all with a political subtext: the miners were essential but troublesome.

You can feel the irritation in a 1958 Cabinet

memorandum on Fuel Policy and Problems, marked 'Top Secret', when the closure of uneconomic pits is discussed. Cutting back on opencast mining, it argues, 'would have the advantage of being a publicly popular move but the disadvantage of weakening the National Coal Board's already precarious finances. The second option (closing pits) would assist the Board financially but would raise social and unemployment problems . . . special unemployment problems are created by the closure of pits owing to the fact that mining is carried on in close-knit communities.'

Plans to shut down the industry that so amazed Orwell had thus been secretly discussed since the 1950s. The move that finally closed the mines was unusual only in that it was so openly declared. In 1973 the UK had full employment – less than 3 per cent of the working population had no job. In 1974, shortly after Edward Heath's Conservative government had fallen – partly thanks to Heath calling a snap election after a strike by the National Union of Mineworkers (NUM) – the *Economist* published a leaked document called the Ridley Report. Drawn up by Nicholas Ridley MP, founding member of the free-market cadre the Selsdon Group, it explained how the next Conservative government would take on the NUM.

The government should choose the field of battle, Ridley argued. Coal stocks should be built up at power stations; plans should be made to import coal from non-union foreign ports; non-union lorry drivers should be recruited by haulage companies; dual coal-oil firing generators should be installed, at great extra cost; union funding should be the subject of legislation to cut off the money supply to the strikers whilst the government would train and equip a large, mobile squad of police, ready to employ riot tactics against violent picketing.

In 1984, the National Coal Board announced the closure of twenty coal mines with the loss of 20,000 jobs. The government had prepared exactly according to the Ridley plan – stockpiling coal, converting some power stations to burn oil and recruiting fleets of road hauliers to transport coal in case sympathetic railwaymen went on strike to support the miners. The miners walked out on 22 March and stayed out for almost a year. Images from that year are embedded in the national psyche – mounted police riding down pickets with truncheons drawn; a clowning miner in a fake policeman's helmet making a young constable laugh; striking miners' families digging for coal on slag heaps; pitched battles and shouting protesters; stern lectures on the evening news . . . Ten people died – six pickets, three teenagers searching for coal and a taxi driver taking a non-striking miner to work.

The sense of solidarity and support that Orwell found – channelled largely through the unions – meant miners helped each other out, in work and outside.

That solidarity hasn't been forgotten – in Barnsley there's a house that looks more like a fortress, with wire frames on the windows and high walls, which belongs to a former strike-breaker. 'If he buys a new car, it gets vandalized,' one ex-miner told me. 'There's some shops that still won't serve him.'

Closing the pits isn't hugely controversial anymore. There seems to be a grudging sense that it had to be done. The equipment in Mick Trueman's modern mine – which might have made money from pits deemed uneconomic by 1960s and 1970s techniques – was resisted by both the government and the miners. Perhaps, if there had been a bailout for the mines, a huge investment of cash to make the pits and the steelworks profitable with modern technology and new management techniques – as happened in, for instance, Germany – we might still have a manufacturing base. Instead, the UK manufacturing sector has shrunk by two-thirds in the past thirty years. In 1950, the UK accounted for more than 10 per cent of global exports. By 2009 that had dwindled to less than 3 per cent. A million people made cars in the UK during the 1960s. By 2009, that declined to 180,000. Just after the Second World War, manufacturing accounted for 40 per cent of the UK economy – now it is just one-tenth, with the service industry at 75.8 per cent. The coalition government hoped a manufacturing boom would pull us out of recession so that we might not be so reliant on the whims of finance, and we might not have such staggering rates of unemployment and debt. Over the summer of 2011, however, industrial production figures unexpectedly slumped.

The great social problem with sacking tens of thousands of miners is that there is almost no other way of employing so many people in such a small space – as so much was underground, a mine would take up a tiny part of the surface compared to the miles of corridors underground. The equivalent might be a skyscraper like Canary Wharf, home to five major banks – little surface space, thousands of jobs.

Of course, with the 2008 banking bailout we did for the bankers what we didn't do for the miners – we invested £850 billion to keep the banks going. If we'd wanted to restructure manufacturing during the 1980s, the money existed. We had tons of the stuff. There are numbers on the Customs and Excise website recording the money flowing into the UK government's coffers from North Sea oil from the year it was discovered.

For the first few years the government raked in tens of millions per year, but as the 1980s approached the figures rose. In 1979, as Margaret Thatcher took power, it was £2.3 billion. At the start of the miner's strike in 1983, it was £8.8 billion. The following year – 1984, the height of the strike – it peaked at

£12 billion. Across the rest of the decade it fell away gradually until, by 1989, there was just £2.3 billion trickling into the Treasury. John Major's troubled government had to muddle through on a billion a year and it was not until 2001 that the numbers really started to rise again – levelling off at £5.3 billion in 2001–2 and staying there until 2005 when it soared again, hitting £9.3 billion and then – as the credit crunch and the banking bailout strike in 2008–9 – it leapt to almost £13 billion.

In 2008, the *Spectator* had former investment banker Martin Vander Weyer attacking Gordon Brown using the Custom and Excise numbers:

Total tax revenues from North Sea oil since flows began have amounted to well over £200 billion: for 2008-9, with oil prices sky-high, the Treasury expects another £9.9 billion. John Hawksworth of PricewaterhouseCoopers argued in a brilliant squib of a paper published in February ('Dude, where's my oil money?') that if all this oil tax had been set aside and invested in government bonds, it might now amount to some £450 billion — which, to put it in perspective, equals total UK tax revenues for 2007–8.

So we had the money, but we spent it. On fuelling tax cuts and temporary booms. And what do we expect if

we left households workless for generations? Ingle
argues:

At any time in history, when Orwell wrote as well
as our time, we can name working class areas
where doctors fear to go, where buses will not go
after dark, and so on. Now that the old industries
that Orwell saw – the mines, the docks and the
steelworks – have gone, it's totally different, totally
different. There are drugs, no prospect of employment and the absence of the discipline that the
factory system and the major industrial sectors
provided. The grandchildren of the men that
Orwell met – there has not been any work for
years. People don't want to move, they want to
stay with their family and they need support, particularly mothers. So how do you explain to
people – if you have this idea; 'Sorry, it is over.'
That was the 100 years you got and now you get
nothing.

I arrived in Wigan the week of the royal wedding of
William and Kate. As you walk out of the station you
face a large pawnshop. Turn left, and you reach Wigan
Pier – a collection of empty commercial lots with a
plaque commemorating the Queen's opening of the
pier in March 1986 and a sign saying 'Wigan Pier – to

let'. If you turn right out of the station you head into the centre of the town along a street lined with small shops and a cluster of pubs and bars.

That day the sun was glorious and people were drinking outside watching council workers busily erecting a giant screen in the middle of the pedestrianized town square – just outside a brand new shopping mall. They were preparing for a street party to mark the wedding. I met Bob and Dorothy – who worked in education – at the Moon Under Water, a chain named after Orwell's essay on the perfect pub. We strolled back to Bob's house, past pound stores, more bars and a line of beautiful regency houses.

'Wigan's all right,' Bob said as we walked. 'There's lots of people here who don't like the cloth cap and whippets image Orwell's book gave us. The town's not that bad – all the two-up two-downs have gone, the air's clean, it's all right.' He paused, thought, shrugged. 'I mean . . . it's getting worse. You see more shops boarded up every day.'

Later, I caught a bus to meet Joe Goringe, chair of Astley and Tyldesley miners' welfare club in Gin Pit village – which is technically still Wigan but some twenty minutes from the town centre. The pits around the village began closing in the 1950s and there was little left by the late 1970s. Today, there are only ten ex-miners left in the club – the rest are locals or newcomers to the modern housing estates that are still being built for couples from Manchester and Liverpool.

Joe's daughter is a nurse and his son was a steelworker – cutting girders and rods for building sites – until the credit crunch laid waste to the building industry. The lad struggled for fourteen months until he found night-shift work as a fork-lift truck driver. Joe had raised them as a single father after his wife left in 1982. The National Coal Board (NCB) had been understanding – his lateness was tolerated but he would still have to have both ready for school by the time he left for work at 6 a.m. When he suffered an ultimately crippling accident, the NCB let him recover on full pay for eighteen months. When he returned to work they let him take the holiday he'd been accruing and finally, when it was clear he would never truly recover, they let him go with a handsome payoff. In the world of sub-contracts, agency jobs and casual contracts, he'd recieve nothing and even struggle to set disability benefit.

At the club I meet Sam Long – now retired and driving a mini-cab – who spent eighteen months down the pit before a cage slipped and he was injured. He got a job as a sterilizing operator at Heinz. He operated the machine that cooked the baked beans – a thirty-five minute process with the beans passing through five chambers where they are steam-cooked. He was a shop steward at Heinz and took redundancy after twenty years. His son followed him into the plant, won an apprenticeship and has been there for thirty years working as an electrician.

'If nothing else I'm glad I worked at Heinz so my son could,' Sam explains. 'Electrician down a mine is no life. Imagine a coalface one foot high and 300 yards long – you're the electrician that has to crawl all the way up the face to change a cable that has been crushed by a roof falling in. You would have to climb over rocks, machines and anything else that was in your path. You'd be carrying a full kit of tools in boiling temperatures and you'd rely on people giving you the correct message about what was wrong so that you would only carry what was needed for the job.

'When you got to the top, if they'd missed anything or got it wrong you'd have to go back down the 300 yards on your knees to get whatever was required. The only food and water that was available was what you carried and if you missed the train into the face then you had to walk three miles carrying everything – tools, food, water, spare parts, everything. But you felt OK compared to the coalface workers. They had to be at the coalface by 7 a.m. so it was down the pit by 6 a.m., which meant travelling to work at 5 a.m. At Heinz you'd be by the machine, steaming hot all day long but you were never going to die. And I was the shop steward, so I went on courses outside the company where people would look at me with envy when I described my job, pay and conditions.'

Now that the pits have gone, the town's big employers are the council, followed by the local hospital trust. Heinz runs the biggest canning plant in northern Europe, near Wigan, producing more than one billion cans of beans and soup a year and employing 1,000 people. All three are threatened – cuts are hitting the council and the health service, while Heinz is threatening to close the plant as part of a restructure.

Hitchen Foods is Wigan's own food-processing plant. Gerald Hitchen started life selling groceries off the back of a horse and cart in the 1930s – according to local legend. Hitchen's moved into wholesale, became a limited company in 1961 and by 2005 – when it was sold to Geest Foods, part of Iceland's Bakkavor Group, for £44 million – employed 750 people making ready-to-eat meals and packaged salads for supermarkets and fast-food chains. With Heinz and five major bakeries in the town, for Wigan food is the new coal.

In the spirit of Orwell, I went for a day shift at the company. The legend about working for Hitchens is that you can show up at reception with your CV and the man on the door can offer you a job on the spot. People with experience, however, told me to go through an agency instead. I found one in the middle of town, where a Polish woman interviewed me for a temporary post as a food production operative.

Most of the questions she asked were about my legal

status to prove I was eligible to work in the UK. There was also a short English test, which included basic safety signs, and I fluffed a few of those questions. She looked at me strangely.

'It's odd, you are English but you got those questions wrong.'

I mumbled awkwardly, 'I think I misunderstood what you were asking.'

She paused for a second, shrugged and gave me the details of my shift – mid-afternoon to midnight, offering the minimum wage of £5.93 per hour.

Each shift would be worth £47 before tax and agency deductions – around £30 after said deductions, meaning a weekly take-home pay of around £150, almost exactly equivalent to the income of the Hornby family with whom Orwell stayed in Warrington Lane. Renting a one-bedroom flat in Wigan starts at roughly £75 per week, a two-bed at roughly £100 per week and a three-bed house at roughly £110. The average rent in Warrington Lane, according to property site Zoopla, is £117 per week – meaning more than half of my pay would go on accommodation.

The Department of Energy and Climate Change estimates that the average weekly fuel bill for a UK household is £60 and rising – I'd be at the low end of that in a one-bed flat but near the top end if I was supporting a family. A single person could perhaps muddle through on £150 per week if they lived carefully – I couldn't see how I could support dependants without running up hefty debts. Hitchen Foods has a poor reputation in the town – the work is hard and monotonous and the low pay doesn't help. A bunch of kids who'd failed GCSEs and were studying for an IT vocational qualification said Hitchen was used as a bogeyman to get them back into education – if you get no qualifications, you'll have to join the people who work at Hitchen Foods.

On a spring day, Hitchen Foods' square, modern factory building with high white walls and angled roofs – surrounded by a high fence and reached via a narrow alley – didn't look too bad. The whole of Ince – although it's got a dubious reputation and is one of the most deprived areas in the UK, with very high rates of incapacity benefit claimants for mental illness and hospital stays for alcohol-related harm – is still less threatening than it used to be.

In *A History of the County of Lancaster* – written in 1911 – Farrer and Brownbill described Ince:

> The general aspect is unpleasing, it being a typical black country in the heart of the coal-mining area. The flat surface, covered with a complete network of railways, has scarcely a green tree to relieve the monotony of the bare wide expanses of apparently wasteland, much of it covered with shallow 'flashes' of water, the result of the gradual

subsidence of the ground as it is mined beneath. A good deal of the ground appears to be unreclaimed mossland. Needless to say no crops are cultivated. All the energies of the populace are employed in the underground mineral wealth of the district, Ince being famous for cannel and other coal.

Today the heavy industry has gone, leaving small industrial units and miles of post-war houses – built, as it turned out, on contaminated soil. Hitchen is on one of the larger estates. I signed in at the reception building with an Eastern European woman in her late thirties who had beetroot-coloured, permed hair. We passed through into the factory. There are four smaller factories inside: Unit 1 processes onion, carrots or potato for ready meals; Unit 2 handles salads, Unit 3 processes mashed products; and Unit 4 prepares jacket potatoes. The whole place smells of boiling root vegetables with occasional whiffs of onion. Every now and then another scent would drift over as a new dish started its chain of cooking or packing.

I was shown to a kit room where they gave me heavy-duty boots, a blue bodysuit, apron, gloves and an elasticated plastic bag to cover my hair. I was told to make sure I was as sealed up as possible – no entry points that might expose my clothes and skin apart from the neck. People who'd worked at Hitchens warned me to wear a fleece underneath – which seemed excessive as I changed and felt little droplets of sweat run across my chest.

My first job, however, was on the salad assembly line – packing leaves into plastic bags in a vast room the size of an aircraft hangar. The air was chilled to protect the produce – salad ingredients stacked high all around the room – and it had a curious quality to it, like being sealed in an air-conditioning unit large enough to fit a house. There were no windows and the lighting was bright and bleak – these are all health and safety measures, but it made me feel as if I was in a giant concrete bunker deep underground. I'd taken my watch off and it was impossible to tell what time of day it was or whether it was light or dark outside.

People kept moving through the room, coming down from the offices located high on an overlooking gantry, or pushing in and out huge trolleys stacked with food – all of them clad in white overalls. The constant movement of antiseptic, anonymous workers felt like a dystopian science-fiction movie although the salad conveyor belt – initially preparing Marks and Spencer salads then switching neatly to Burger King – could have come from any film about the mindless repetition of mechanized labour.

The conveyor belt constantly moved forwards. One worker placed empty plastic cartons on to trays, the rest added ingredients – mine was the sachets of dressing –

with the final worker sealing it up and adding a label. The team were very nimble, stuffing and wrapping within seconds as the completed salads stacked at the end. I quickly discovered that my speed and dexterity were way below the rest of the production line and I was soon holding up the line as I reached for fresh sachets. I could feel the slight air of tension as I created tiny problems and delays. Nobody spoke – no greetings, no questions about the weekend or last night's telly – and I wasn't sure if this was a rule, a language issue or just sheer boredom.

I kept giving apologetic looks to the woman further up the line from me. She looked Eastern European but I wasn't sure. I wondered if she spoke much English and how she had ended up in this factory on the edge of Wigan. Her brief glances back were blank: depression or boredom or a complete lack of interest. Eventually I was moved to the top of the line and, after a few bumbling attempts, a man showed me how to get the salad trays ready. He steadied them on his hand – rather than the 'cradling a baby' stance I had improvised – and then he seemed to slide into a state of constant motion, no move wasted, every action nimble and deliberate.

I tried to copy him, and gradually got faster – relaxing slightly and allowing my mind to wander. I suddenly found I was hungry. I was briefly surprised – for the first couple of hours I'd felt slightly sick. I tried to guess what the time might be and stole an occasional glance at the huge overhead storage bins piled high with salad leaves. I wondered how much could still be left in them.

Eventually the silos were spent and they gave me a giant brush, which opened out like scissors, to sweep the salad debris from the factory floor. The ground was littered with prawns and strips of lettuce, and the water that drizzled down to help wash everything away lifted the smell of prawn to my nose, causing me to gag briefly. I swept the brown mulch harder and harder, my back aching, amazed at how hard it was to scrub the floor clean.

Suddenly a man yelled down from the gantry – where were my earplugs? I'd thought they were optional, I explained, worried that I was already known as the difficult agency worker who couldn't work the salad line. He mumbled darkly about health and safety regulations and compensation. Oddly, standing in the middle of the chilled room, I felt grateful for health and safety regulations. The idea that someone would reach into this place and tell management to make sure my ears were OK was comforting – I was already feeling lost but if things went badly wrong I felt there would be someone keeping tabs.

They moved me to the potatoes – many, many potatoes. I was taken aback by the sheer volume. They seemed to rain down the shoot from the roof. My job was to bag these up and then to place them in a skip on wheels. The other men in this part of the factory were local and seemed much more relaxed than the women on the salad line. Every now and then the potato dispenser would shudder to a halt and technicians would climb up and restore it to operation. As we waited, they'd mess around with an Eastern European guy, teaching him obscene hand gestures.

When the potatoes were bagged and stacked, a supervisor told one of the men to take me to the back of the factory to build cardboard boxes. My new colleague was like an origami master – he lifted and assembled flat packs into 3D creations before my eyes, almost chopping at the box in mid-flow, like placing spin on a table-tennis ball. I managed an approximation of his technique, although I struggled to produce boxes with a perfectly flat bottom – necessary to fully support its hefty contents.

Finally, I had a lunch break. I desperately wanted to rest my tired body and get some visual relief from the nightmarish stacks of food piled all around me. The canteen was like a standard school refectory – long tables with men gathered in groups. A few, like me, ate alone. I went for the sweetest snacks available – anything that didn't remind me of the jobs downstairs. In the end, for the energy of the sugar rush, I chose a Coke and a Mars bar. I caught snatches of conversation about the weekend's football. The refectory seemed so intimately related to the factory floor that once I had eaten there seemed little comfort in hanging around.

I shrugged back into my boots and suit and headed back to the box area. This second stint didn't seem so daunting. I began talking to the man working alongside me – the box magician. He was from Croydon and had worked here for nearly five years. He had moved to Wigan thanks to a girlfriend, he said. I got the impression that the relationship was over. I asked why he was still at Hitchen. He had his contract, he said; he knew what to do and could come in, switch off and collect his pay packet.

He had me pegged as a temp and didn't seem interested in conversation. The talking merged with the whirr of forklifts turning and the sound of steam jets from distant parts of the factory. I began filling our boxes with sliced apple packs for Burger King. I now had a rhythm and was trying to put a pack in a box then moving the next one into position before I had time to think. I found myself humming the Johnny Cash song 'Get Rhythm': 'Get rhythm, when you get the blues, come on, get rhythm . . .'

Someone stopped, watched me for a second and remarked that I was a good worker. I felt grateful and grabbed more boxes, keen to impress. Suddenly a loud bell went, a man looked over and called me to him. I was on rubbish duty. I felt slightly deflated. Had my deft box-packing not been fast enough? He didn't react, just passed me on to a foreign worker, who took charge.

We collected white strapping tape from the floor as a man slashed it from the packaging of large boxes with a Stanley knife, which he kept in his hip pocket. We were to take it to one of the waste disposal bins – large plastic wheeled skips. I tried to make conversation – cracking a weak joke about the skip as we stuffed tape into it. He nodded and threw in the strapping he held, and then returned to work in silence.

My supervisor from the box area returned with a senior-looking colleague and told us the shift was over. He looked at me. There was more work available, he said, if I wanted it. I shrugged and said yes, unsure if he meant now or extra shifts that week. He pointed to the door and told my fellow rubbish-packer he could go – I would get the overtime. The guy turned and walked away without a trace of emotion.

As I continued working I wondered if he needed the extra hours' money more than me. I thought of the docks, men lined up and picked out of a line on an arbitrary basis for a day's work. I wondered if they'd deliberately picked the Englishman.

My body was aching and I felt weak as the next shift arrived and started working around me, starting a full night at the plant (Hitchen runs twenty-four hours a day) – it was as if I only had the energy for the eight hours and I'd spent it all bang on time. Extra work seemed physically impossible – although I was acutely aware I wasn't hacking a rock face with a pick axe as Orwell's miners had.

All the same, relief flooded through me as I finished. I returned my borrowed clothes to the locker room. I noticed for the first time that some lockers had stickers – personalized lockers owned by full-timers. I walked out into the night air and starlight, and back on to the main road.

I walked alone. I'd met no one from Ince in the factory. When I got back to my bed-and-breakfast – at £29 per night an unaffordable luxury residence on my pay cheque – I shut my eyes and saw mushrooms falling. It had been hard, lonely, repetitive work – it wasn't as dangerous, backbreaking or unhealthy as coal-mining; my life was never in danger – but that doesn't mean it's a life. The GCSE kids had told me to look out for onion ladies – women who chopped all day long in the onion room whose skin was swollen and red after years of getting smeared in the chemical irritant produced by the bulb – syn-propanethial-S-oxide.

Certainly health and safety standards at the Hitchen factory were far, far higher than down the pit in 1936. Even today, it's a hard business digging coal. Paul, a smartly dressed twentysomething sipping his Guinness in a Bradford bar on a Sunday night, left college at seventeen because his mate offered him a job at the last working pit in West Yorkshire – dangling the prospect of a stake in the company over time.

He found it tough. 'Whatever a miner tells you, it's a lousy job.' He shakes his head. 'I don't know a single miner that wouldn't take a decent redundancy package if it was offered.' He left barely a year later – not, he was at pains to point out, because the work was too hard but because a friend was dynamiting coal and blew part of his own face off by accident. 'Health and safety shut us down for a while, it were costing £6,000 a week just to keep the air and pumps going so I couldn't see my share being worth very much.'

Paul travelled out to New Zealand with another ex-miner and found work on a farm in the middle of nowhere, shearing sheep, while his mate shipped over to Sydney. He was homesick and when his grand-parents told him that Henry, the smiley-faced vacuum cleaner company, was recruiting in their Somerset village, his loneliness propelled him back.

'I went for the job at Henry, but you couldn't apply direct,' he explains. 'You had to go through an agency. Then you find you're not really employed by Henry, you're employed by the agency. They didn't have anything for me after three months, and there's nothing else to do in Chard. It's like a pit town. If the pit's not employing, there is no work.'

And so he returned to Bradford where he lived, he says, 'destitute' for a while. But he wasn't alone.

Bradford was once a mill town but during the 1960s and 1970s Britain's cotton mills, the inspiration for and backbone of the Industrial Revolution, closed at the rate of one a week. By the 1980s, the cotton industry had vanished. 'If you've been unemployed for three months, no one round here wants to know,' Paul said. 'I'd go for jobs at a call centre, they'd say – "Your CV says you were a miner. What do you know about customer care?" I'd say, "I'm a bright lad, I can pick it up." They wouldn't be interested.'

In the end he got work at Grattan's catalogue call centre, thanks to a scheme in which the council and Job Centre paid his salary for the first six months. Plenty of people lost their jobs soon after the subsidy dried up, but he'd stayed on – he's been there for two years now, taking home roughly £200 per week, although he can earn a £1 bonus for each call whereby he manages to persuade a customer to purchase something they hadn't been planning to buy.

'There's order calls, a lot of complaint calls, and then checking up on orders,' he explains. 'You've got different systems for logging orders and calls, urgent requests, and accounts – everything really, and you have to switch between them all the time. So if someone rings up with a complaint you've got to turn it around and sell them something within nine minutes switching between these different systems – inbound sales training. You get maybe ten seconds between calls

– so it's stressful sometimes but it's better than working in the Santander call centre up the road, because that's financial services. You have a script there and everything's recorded because what you say – if you fuck it up there's legal implications. At least at Grattan I can use the words I want, within reason.'

If he can't turn any deals around and only earns his £200 per week basic wage, Paul comes in below the Minimum Income Standard of £240.89 per week for single adults of working age, as defined by the Joseph Rowntree Foundation. This standard – updated every year, most recently in July 2011 – is 'the income that people need in order to reach a minimum socially acceptable standard of living in the United Kingdom today, based on what members of the public think.'

Every year since the project began in 2008, the foundation asks a series of focus groups – typically six to eight people per group – to describe the things they feel a family would have to be able to afford to achieve an acceptable life: food, drink, shelter, social life and so on. There are four family types – single working age person, pensioner couple, a couple with two children and a lone parent with one child. Each group's basket of goods – the minimum expectations list – is drawn up by a group of peers. In other words, single people decide on the list for single people and pensioners for pensioners.

Once everyone has agreed on their list, experts weigh

in to check the findings are reasonable – that the food meets basic nutritional needs, for example, and the life promised walks the difficult but eminently reasonable line between basic subsistence and unnecessary extravagance. The list covers needs, not wants, necessities, not luxuries. According to the report's author, Donald Hirsch: 'A minimum standard of living in Britain today includes, but is more than just, food, clothes and shelter. It is about having what you need in order to have the opportunities and choices necessary to participate in society.'

In 2011, Hirsch concluded, a single person needed to earn at least £15,000 a year before tax to afford a minimum acceptable standard of living whilst a couple with a single earner and two children needed at least £31,600. The numbers follow categories set out by the government's basket of goods and services used to calculate inflation and, for the Joseph Rowntree Foundation, they break down like this:

Single working adult
£46.31 per week for food
£4.96 for alcohol
Nothing for tobacco, which would have
    infuriated Orwell
£8.56 for clothes
£5.16 for water rates
£13.95 for council tax

£2 for household insurance

£10.51 for fuel

£2.48 for other housing costs

£10.99 for household goods – furniture, bedding, TV, etc.

£4.53 for household services – cleaning and fixing stuff

Nothing for childcare

£9.34 for personal goods and services – anything from toothpaste to painkillers

Nothing for motoring, which would infuriate Jeremy Clarkson

£22.17 for other travel

£43.71 for social and cultural participation – a loose grouping that includes the Retail Piece Index's recreational, cultural and sporting services

£56.21 for rent

Paul seems surprised by the list. He thought he'd got a bit of a deal on his rent – £56 a week was low, he explained, and he'd got it thanks to blagging his housing association bedsit. The idea that this was pretty much bang on the minimum standard of living rent bothered him. He'd been struggling a bit financially – a little bit of debt, nothing he couldn't handle – but his rent deal had comforted him as he sat in the vast warehouse surrounded by old people and students, thinking himself a man on the way up but unsure how to move on.

The same is true for twenty-four-year-old Kaine Said, from the Canterbury Estate in Bradford. He's been a general building labourer for close to two years. His role is to assist the plumbers, bricklayers, electricians, plasterers – anyone with a skill or a trade. With money being so tight and demarcation a long-dead concept, the specialists guard their skill jealously, desperate to avoid creating young, fresh competition.

If Said asks too many questions about what the tradesmen are doing, or if they think he is paying too much attention to the minutiae of the job, they square up to him, telling him to back off, to walk away and know his place.

Every couple of weeks he has to pitch for work all over again – sometimes every week. It feels like the infamous dockers' pit outside Liverpool docks, where casual hands gathered every morning in the hope of a day shift, sometimes offering bribes to supervisors so they could be picked for hours of back-breaking work.

'I'll get offered a job for a month – they always tell you a month, always, but when you get there it's a week or two, so when it's over I run down to the resource centre and ring all the agencies, like 100 agencies, asking what's coming up.' Said gives a grin. 'OK, not 100, but loads. Agencies pay you a week in hand – so I get a wage the week after I work. I never want to be facing a week without a wage coming in so I call around and around. You get the thing where suddenly three people come back with a better rate but you've already taken something and you can't turn a job down once you've taken it or you'll never work for that agency again. Usually you get between £6 to £8 an hour. Last week I was on £7.60 for days and £8 for nights.'

'Depending on the shift?' I ask. There's a pause. We fail to understand each other. He twigs first. 'No, I mean I was doing double shifts,' he explains. 'I was on a twelve-hour night shift at a site building a new Sainsbury's in Halifax, 7 p.m. to 7 a.m., then the bus to Leeds for an 8 a.m. start, finishing at 4.30 p.m. I'd be nodding off on the bus or sleeping in the canteen. But I hate what I do, so I'm saving up for a course in Birmingham and just kept thinking about that. It was only five days. Now I'm on £6.65 day shifts.'

For this epic feat of endurance and willpower, Said earned a total of £480 for the week on nights and £304 for the days – which would give him an annual salary of around £40,820, slightly more than the £40,000 starting salary for a graduate trainee at supermarket chain Aldi. Admittedly, this is a slightly unfair comparison. Aldi offer significantly more than other firms because they have a very high graduate burnout rate. Recruits work seventy hours or more each week, including working on both Saturday and Sunday, sometimes for months at a time. (Even so, it's a job. In

2010, each trainee post had over 12,000 applicants.)

Of course, it would be impossible to maintain twenty-hour days, so Said's peak earning power in realistic terms is £480 per week or £24,950 per year – that's if he's working twelve-hour shifts, taking no holidays and having no days off sick. At £6.65 per hour, his rate is below the average hourly pay rate for someone with no qualifications at all – in 2010, according to the Office for National Statistics, that was £6.93. The average wage for those with higher grade GCSEs (As to Cs) is £8.68 per hour – Said's qualifications after he dropped out of an A level course in music and technology at a local college. The average wage for those with A levels was £10 per hour, and a degree earned £16.10 per hour.

Out of his woefully low wages, Said sometimes has to pay his travel costs – he works across West Yorkshire and has even had jobs in Scotland. He always has to provide his own food. He considers himself lucky in that, half the time, agencies will help with travel and, so far, he hasn't worked for an agency that runs its own bus service and charges employees to use it – something he knows is very common.

Said is a hard-working, personable man fervently hoping to better himself. The course for which he's saving up is a week-long residential course in Birmingham that'll give him a licence to operate steam rollers, dumper trucks and cherry pickers – meaning he'll earn £10 an hour and possibly work contracts up to six-months' long, which should mean an annual salary of £30,000. The course costs £1,700, however, so he's had to move out of his flat into a bedsit and rely on his family for food.

In other words, not only does the employer use an agency to avoid paying sick or holiday wages, they have – in effect – contracted out every aspect of Said's job that isn't actual physical labour, including his training, his food and his travel. It used to be the case that an employer would take care of almost everything – and would certainly bear the cost of training through apprenticeships or in-house schemes, figuring that better-equipped staff would be more productive. In the case of towns such as Bourneville, just outside Birmingham, and Port Sunlight, near Wirral, Cadbury and Unilever paid for sporting facilities and cultural institutes. Joe Goringe chairs a miner's institute built on land donated to the miners by their employers (the mines were privately owned) at the height of the 1926 general strike – the men were in dispute with the mining company yet it still gave them a parcel of land.

Today, it's the other way around. Companies take care of our purchasing needs from cradle to grave – Tesco and Morrisons will sell you car insurance, books, clothing, electronics, furniture, petrol, software, phones and music downloads. Apprenticeships are thin on the ground, but with university fees about to soar, supermarkets are helping undergraduates a little. In spring 2011, for instance, Morrisons announced plans to fund business degrees at Bradford University – specializing in retail management. Students on the three-year course, which started in September 2011, spend most of their time on the shop floor and will have employee holidays, rather than university holidays, for which they will receive £15,000 per year and have their fees paid.

Imad Faghmous, academic affairs officer for Bradford University's students union, said the new degree course offered a fantastic opportunity to students worried about money: 'In a situation where funding is decreasing, we're going to see a lot more of the private sector stepping in to help students.'

He's right. In 2010 Harrods announced it was to offer two-year degrees in sales with Anglia Ruskin University; GlaxoSmithKline announced it would sponsor a module on University of Nottingham chemistry degrees – the first collaboration of its kind between a pharmaceutical company and a university; while Tesco sponsors a pre-degree foundation course in retail with Manchester Metropolitan University and University of the Arts London.

Said is resolutely cheerful in the face of all his hard work. At least, he says, he knows the hours he's going to work each day – he's always told the length of the shift so that even if the contract is far shorter than promised he can estimate his daily take-home pay. He's also grateful to be earning so much. The Eastern Europeans on site, he explains, work as hard as him for £3 or £4 per hour. One man I met at Hitchens worked a thirty-hour week and took home £30. One of his deductions – taken by the agency – was for 'other'. And, because he is Eastern European, he's been attacked three times since he was in Wigan for taking local jobs.

Even these conditions are gradually becoming a luxury. The past few years have seen the rise of zero-hour contracts – a full employment contract that guarantees you nothing. There was some fuss when Burger King and car company Daewoo began introducing zero-hour contracts in the mid-1990s – Burger King ultimately paid £106,000 in compensation to nearly 900 employees who were asked to clock off during slack periods in 1996. Now these contracts are commonplace.

Robin Tenant works at Argos, in Warrington. 'They gave me a four-hour contract – it only guarantees four hours work a week,' he explains. 'Now for some people it suits them absolutely fine, do you know? Four hours work a week if you were a pensioner trying to top up your pension or you're just starting going back to work is fine. But we are a family and both me and my partner have a four-hour contract with one store and so we have eight hours work between us for a week. We're employed, so we don't have . . . so unemployment benefit becomes a complete nightmare because we technically have contracts and we may have thirty-six hours work one week and then four and it means that as soon as something happens – like, just the week before Christmas last year the snow happened – we're stuffed. We'd been thinking that's a fine, busy period. I'll bank on those two weeks – I'll use my staff discount and I'll have paid for Christmas. Then, when the snow happened, no one went into town so the store sent everyone home with four hours work at the minimum wage. I mean what's that? £28 a week? It's not enough to live.'

'One of the big narratives is that work is good for people,' says Helen Longworth of Oxfam. 'It gives them security, it gives them balance. Although actually, for a lot of people now it's not giving them anything, it's not even giving them work most of the time. They have a contract but they can't earn any money and because they have a contract they can't claim benefits. They need a set of contracts to guarantee at least some work. The first hour's work pays for the bus fare and then you have to go to another job to see if you can work that day. You're creating a shift pattern with no responsibility on the employer and no duty of care on that employer to make sure that you and your family are okay. It's not giving people a reason to come out of the house. They're just getting a phone call on a Monday morning saying – yeah, we don't need you, sorry, sales figures are down.'

CHAPTER 3

Money

Even when I am on the verge of starvation I have certain rights attaching to my bourgeois status. I do not earn much more than a miner earns, but I do at least get it paid into my bank in a gentlemanly manner and can draw it out when I choose. And even when my account is exhausted the bank people are passably polite. This business of petty inconvenience and indignity, of being kept waiting about, of having to do everything at other people's convenience, is inherent in working-class life. A thousand influences constantly press a working man down into a passive role. He does not act, he is acted upon.

George Orwell, *The Road to Wigan Pier*, 1936

I ask you, what am I? I'm one of the undeserving

poor: that's what I am. Think of what that means to a man. It means that he's up against middle class morality all the time. If there's anything going, and I put in for a bit of it, it's always the same story: 'you're undeserving; so you can't have it.' But my needs is as great as the most deserving widow's that ever got money out of six different charities in one week for the death of the same husband. I don't need less than a deserving man: I need more. I don't eat less hearty than him; and I drink a lot more. I want a bit of amusement, cause I'm a thinking man. I want cheerfulness and a song and a band when I feel low. Well, they charge me just the same for everything as they charge the deserving. What is middle class morality? Just an excuse for never giving me anything. Therefore, I ask you, as two gentlemen, not to play that game on me. I'm playing straight with you. I ain't pretending to be deserving. I'm undeserving and I mean to go on being undeserving. I like it; and that's the truth.

George Bernard Shaw, Alfred Doolittle in
Pygmalion, 1912

'I believe that you live each day as it comes, shall I tell you for why?' Peter from Bradford tells me. 'Because at nineteen years old, the mother of my first child, Sharon – I were walking down to her house for my tea and I walked into her road – which is a massive dual carriageway leading out of Bradford – and a car comes straight through the red lights and smashed me. I were in intensive care for about five weeks. I had bit me tongue off, I had head injuries, I had metal plates put in my legs and I were in hospital for six months until I could walk. I come out of intensive, and I thought, "Jesus, what have I done with my life? I could have been dead."

'I worked for nineteen years – I only ever had two jobs. Ten years up Brigella Mills up Loughton Lane and ten years at Stylo Barretts on nights loading articulated wagons. It were all good labour until they sacked me in 1997. I've not had a job since. I've got six kids with three different mothers but I'm now single – I've not been one to settle down. But the main thing is each mother I'm friends with and all my children are brilliant.

'To be quite honest I've always thought – if I die tomorrow . . . well, I'll tell you the truth, I've got cirrhosis of the liver. I were diagnosed three years ago. I don't touch alcohol now, believe you me, but it were a shock. The first six months I did cut down, I just drank shandy. But I had a smoke as well. And then when I went to see the doctor, he knew. He said, "Peter, I'm not kidding you, you carry on drinking, you'll be dead within six months to two years." If I stay off alcohol, I'm forty-seven, I could live up to the age of fifty-five, which is pretty good. I want to go to fifty, because I don't want to die before my mother. End of. I want to make sure I'm here. If I die before me mother, she'll die straight after me. My mam is mentally ill, she's on medication because she tried to commit suicide about ten years ago. I got her to a crash unit it's called. They fought for her for nearly eight hours to keep her alive. So end of the day, I've got to be strong for everybody.'

When I met Peter, he burst into the room with the energy and enthusiasm of a teenager on a big night out, full of life and laughter. He's the kind of person it's fun just to be around. Yes, he fits the image of Alfred Doolittle – whenever I spoke to people about how small the numbers of idle layabouts were, even by official figure, they'd say, 'Ah, but those people *are* out there.' Peter, by Doolittle's measure, is one of the undeserving poor. He's unemployed, spent years drinking and has children by three different women. He fits the image, but that image is largely mythical. Applying it to the vast majority of unemployed, low-waged or benefit-claiming Brits is an entirely unfair comparison.

In terms of alcohol consumption, for instance, the poorer you are the less you drink – which has been true for years and years in survey after survey. Women in professional households or who work full-time are the most likely to exceed recommended weekly limits, whilst men who are employers or managers or earning over £500 a week tend to drink more than other men. There's also a difference in the type of alcohol, with wines and spirits more likely to be quaffed by the middle class whilst beer consumption, a less potent form of boozing is higher among the working class. And yet, for all the low intake and lower alcohol levels, it's men in deprived inner-city areas who tend to die from alcohol-related illness.

The phrase 'the undeserving poor' – defining the difference between those who deserve charity and those who, through their own inferiority, deserve to be poor – dates back to Elizabethan times. Karl Marx offers a more colourful description: 'This scum of the depraved elements of all classes . . . decayed roués, vagabonds, discharged soldiers, discharged jailbirds, escaped galley slaves, swindlers, pickpockets, tricksters, gamblers, brothel keepers, beggars, the dangerous class, the social scum, that passively rotting mass thrown off by the lowest layers of the old society.'

At the moment, in the UK, being poor is based on income alone. There's no moral agenda. But it's on its way. Will Hutton supports 'remoralizing' the welfare debate 'not around the universal principle, but about the principle of deservingness'. Influential Conservative commentator Tim Montgomerie – who worked closely with Iain Duncan Smith on developing today's government welfare policy – dislikes phrases like undeserving poor but thinks 'the best sort of language of welfare . . . says that if you do the right thing, we will support you'.

Orwell preferred Peter from Bradford's principles:

> When people live on the dole for years at a time they grow used to it, and drawing the dole, though it remains unpleasant, ceases to be shameful. But they don't necessarily lower their standards by cutting out luxuries and concentrating on necessities; more often it is the other way about – the more natural way, if you come to think of it. Hence the fact that in a decade of unparalleled depression, the consumption of all cheap luxuries has increased.

These days, there's a new definition of undeserving poor entering our lexicon – the undeserving poor who have refrigerators and colour TVs. In a bar in the centre of Liverpool, I was talking to two rangy twenty-somethings about the difficulties of getting a job if you're from Toxteth. 'You can apply for a job, get an interview, but when they see that you live in postcode L8, they're not interested,' one was saying when a man in his late forties, looking furious, butted in from the end of the table.

'As a social worker I have been in the most deprived areas of this city and they've all got heating, colour TV, computers, mobile phones and money,' he almost spluttered. 'What they're all doing with it is wasting money on alcohol, tobacco, drugs, gambling and ready meals with low nutritional value.' A little later, he actually said: 'Not one of the people that came out of the concentration camps alive was fat. Put these gross people in solitary confinement with 500 calories a day for a few weeks, they would have no problem with their weight gain then.' It's possible he was simply winding us up.

'Words like chav are basically a smokescreen for class hatred,' argues Owen Jones, author of *Chavs: The Demonisation of the Working Class*, when I interviewed him. 'The idea of the undeserving is really important in an unequal society – it means the poor are poor because it's their fault and the rich are at the top because they deserve to be. It died out in Britain for a while, but you see it coming back from the 1980s on. It usually comes with the idea that the poor have to be starving to be called poor. The fact that TV sets are cheap and people can borrow money easily doesn't seem to have occurred to people who are horrified when the working class take part in consumer culture. That's why you now get "Chav Free Holidays" and Burberry is horrified that the wrong sort of people like its clothes.'

It's very hard to calculate how much the state pays out to your average middle-class suburban family compared to an inner-city family on benefits, but one thing is clear: the poor make a lot of people very, very rich. I met Wilf, a commercial property expert, in a bar in Wigan, who talked about 'The Pound Wars' – the name he gave to the frantic bidding for prime spots to sell to the very poor – Poundland, Pound World, Home Choice and BrightHouse all try to outbid each other for the right part of a depressed northern town. 'You look at the rents these chains are offering to pay – top, top rents – and you think, how can they make any money? Their customers are all living in poverty, but the poor spend. You get the cheque in on Thursday and it's gone by Friday.'

He gives a guilty shrug. He's from a deprived part of Mansfield, but his property deals have helped exploit the people he left behind. He helped secure a grant from a council in northwest England to encourage a small factory to relocate to an industrial estate – the council even built new roads. When the factory owner, a local man who'd set up down south to take advantage of the asylum-seeker processing centre in Hastings, finally arrived he brought most of his Polish workforce with him. He provided the bare minimum in terms of local jobs – meeting exactly the terms laid out in the contract but no more.

'What really gets me is how people make money out of working-class sports,' Wilf reflects. 'Someone like Dave Whelan, the guy who owned JJB Sports when it got caught price-fixing football shirts back in 2005. He owned Wigan Warriors then and still owns Wigan Athletic now. seventy thousand watch Wigan every week and shirts cost £70. He was selling the shirts twice at one point – as club owner and as shop. When I did business with him, Whelan used to go through the building switching off toilet lights to save money, regardless of whether they were occupied.'

Getting the poor to pay over the odds for something is big business. Save the Children calls it the poverty premium – the higher prices the poorest families often pay for basic necessities such as gas, electricity and banking. The charity estimates the poverty premium costs around £1,280 per seat for a typical low-income family. And this has risen by over £280 since the original research in 2007 – much faster than inflation.

According to the Institute of Fiscal Studies, the top 20 per cent of earners in the UK faced overall inflation of 2.5 per cent between 2008 and 2010 whilst the poorest one-fifth experienced inflation of 4.3 per cent. Essential purchases, including food and fuel, account for a much larger proportion of spending by poorer people and it is petrol and food that have seen some of the biggest price rises in recent years – while interest payments for the average mortgage have fallen. But it's also down to high tariffs on prepayment meters or cards for gas and electricity, not being able to afford household insurance, buying shoddy goods at a premium price because you can't afford to shop elsewhere, or having so little you have to borrow at extortionate rates. Item for item, it costs more to be poor.

'It's not easy feeding four kids on benefits,' says Geoff, who lives in a three-bedroom house in Mansfield with his partner Tannie. 'We try to get them to eat their five a day because, you know, we lost babies in the past,' he pauses and they both look at the ground. 'Cot death.' There's a long pause. I half expect them to take each other's hands, or make contact in some physical, reassuring way, but they seem alone. In the end, he raises his eyes while she keeps looking at the floor.

'But vegetables, they've gone up, milk, that's gone up, ham for lunch, we used to pay 80p per packet, now it's £1.40 odd. So our food is doubling but the money is the same so we're borrowing. I'm worried about the debt. I want the kids to get a job – I make sure they go to school every day. I just want them to grow up and get a nice car, house, partner, you know. I don't want them to be stuck like we are. I've always wanted to be an electrician or mechanic, get a mortgage. We're stuck on these benefits not through choice.' He looks at Tannie briefly, just for a second, then back to me. 'I've got to look after the children.'

Debt is widespread. People owe money to landlords, utility companies, family and friends, credit card companies and banks. Doorstep lenders are ever-present and persistent, especially when people are at their most vulnerable. Borrowing money can be crippling on a low income. Those households often have a poor or non-existent credit history and struggle to get a bank account, let alone borrow from banks and building societies.

Often the only option available is rent-to-buy, catalogues or doorstep lenders such as Mutual, Shop-A-Check, CLC Finance, Norton Finance and Loans For You who charge high interest rates on goods and mark-up on retail prices. The annual percentage rate charged by these lenders, Save the Children found, can vary from 50 to 1,000 per cent, compared with less than 30 per cent APR charged by a mainstream lender. One site, Wonga.com, which provides quick cash loans for a short time, has an APR of 4,214 per cent.

Provident Financial is possibly the largest of these doorstep lenders. It has over 11,400 agents – 72 per cent are women – and they're paid on a commission basis. A £500 loan from the Provident means paying back £910 at an APR of 272.2 per cent. People borrow for the little things – food and kids clothes, racking up debts for everyday items. Agents offer fresh loans a couple of weeks before old loans are paid off and – although technically they are not supposed to let loans stack up – are quite happy to run two or three loans side by side. They're paid on commission, after all.

Provident calls this 'serving the 10 million plus non-standard credit market'. The company's pre-tax profits for the first six months of 2011 were £62.3 million – up 15 per cent on 2010. Financial results are incredibly dull to read – one reason my interview for a job as a reporter on the financial pages of the *Daily Telegraph* ten years ago went so badly wrong. But there are always people at the heart of the balance sheet. Provident's hugely successful financial results link two groups of people: the 2.4 million desperately poor who have to borrow short-term cash loans on their doorstep at enormous interest rates (a number slightly larger than the population of Paris or Toronto); and Provident's shareholders who, with corporation tax falling from 28 per cent to 26 per cent in April, saw their earnings rise 16 per cent.

This difficulty in borrowing from mainstream banks and building societies means that a basic household cooker can cost a low-income family more than two-and-a-half times the cost of the same cooker bought outright.

Basic household item prices and the poverty premium

Typical cooker price: £239.00. Cost to low-income family: £669.24

Typical charge to cash 3 x £200 cheques: £0. Cost to low-income family: £36.00

Typical annual electricity and gas bill combined: £881.06. Low income: £1,134.23

Typical home contents insurance: £66.72. Low
  income: £98.64
Typical car insurance: £309.82. Low income:
  £597.96
Source: Save the Children

The extra cost of gas and electricity for low-income
families accounts for 20 per cent of the poverty
premium. Across social housing and low-income
homes, families often pay for their gas and electricity
using prepayment meters, thus paying one of the
highest tariffs on offer – the lowest tariffs are offered to
customers who can pay by direct debit online, so low-
income families without a bank account are automatically excluded. Five of the big six energy companies
don't include families with children on their lower-cost
social tariffs.

In the last six years, gas and electricity bills have
more than doubled – and the increases aren't stopping
anytime soon. Any across-the-board increase has the
biggest impact on those paying the highest tariffs – in
other words, those using prepayment meters. Fuel
poverty is defined as households who have to spend
more than 10 per cent of their income on fuel. Ofgem
estimates that there are five million people in fuel
poverty in the UK, roughly 18 per cent of all households. In the UK, 7 per cent of single parents and 9.9
per cent of couples with children live in fuel poverty.

Alice, a single parent who lives in Doncaster, shifted from a prepayment meter to a conventional billing system and found weekly gas payments of £30 to £40 plummeting to £10. 'It was worse than feeding a donkey in the garden, that gas machine. It was just robbing me blind. How could I be putting £40 in a week to that meter yet I can manage on £10 a week here and it's fine? Something's up, there, don't you think?'

Then there are the loan sharks. Over Christmas 2009, the Financial Inclusion Centre found that 100,000 families had borrowed a total of £29 million from illegal moneylenders. The think tank said on average it would take a year to pay the money back, with lenders recouping three times the value of their loan using interest rates as high as 1,500 per cent.

At one time the Beech Hill estate in Wigan had a lot of problems with doorstep lenders. Before chip-and-pin benefit payments, sharks used to take the family allowance book, meet women outside the post office and hand it to them, then the woman would go in and get money, come out and hand the book back with the money. In Speke, in Liverpool, the loan sharks moved to the estates along with the people who were uprooted from places such as Toxteth. Some loan-sharks families are now in their third generation.

But there's something that riles Eileen Devaney, who runs the Speke Citizens Advice Bureau, even more than loan sharks – BrightHouse, the UK's largest rent-to-buy store. The company sells furniture, electrical equipment and kitchen appliances to customers on low incomes and supplies the credit enabling them to make the purchases. Most of its customers are women – nearly half are largely or wholly dependent on benefits and about two-fifths are single mothers.

BrightHouse traces its roots to Crazy George's — a chain that, in turn, was part of Boxclever, a business formed in the 1999 merger between Granada's television rentals division and Radio Rentals, the two leading companies in the market.

'I've had times when someone hasn't been able to make the payments, they've been outside the door shouting all over the street that you owe this money and you owe that money.' She's grim-faced at the memory. 'And people are holed up, they lock the door. We had a problem with BrightHouse where the manager was threatening to come round the house and take this woman's TV. We told her they couldn't do that, and we spoke to them for her. The woman who was the manager at BrightHouse actually said – "We're not negotiating with you but we'll send our people round to see you." I phoned back, said "I'm the Citizens Advice manager, I believe you're sending some people round." She says, "Yeah, we'll be sending them right over." I said we've got our own security firm here. Why don't I put them in touch with your security firm and they can sort it out together?"' She gives a little laugh. 'We didn't hear from her again.'

BrightHouse, for instance, sells a Samsung 46-inch screen in LED HD 3DTV at £14.62 per week over three years – meaning a total of £2,280.72 (or £3,508.44 with service cover) for a TV available on Amazon for £1,014.90. Of course, to get on to Amazon's website, you need a computer, such as the Acer Gold 15.6 in laptop, which PC World sells for £529.98. If you took 104 easy weekly payments with BrightHouse, it would cost you £742.56 – or with service cover £1,142.96. BrightHouse also has a £3 late payment charge per item – payable the following week alongside a doubling of your original late payment. In other words, if you've got three items – a fridge, a TV and a sofa – you're paying £20 per week and if you miss a payment, the following week you have to pay £49.

An extended warranty direct from Acer for a 15.4 in laptop at the end of the manufacturer's twelve-month guarantee period costs £49.99 for two years – meaning three years cover in all. This includes collection and return, all parts and labour, repairs within five days or a brand new replacement product if not completed within twenty-eight days. Caversham Finance – trading as BrightHouse – offers service cover in 104 weekly payments of £5.95, totalling £618.80 for the two-year duration of the agreement. As Acer guarantee all new products for the first twelve months regardless, this actually only represents one year of extended service cover. Most of the people I spoke to about BrightHouse who had sent goods back for repair had to wait weeks for it to be fixed. BrightHouse makes the assumption that you're taking service cover and so you have to actively opt out at the time of the first agreement to ensure you don't pay it. The company also automatically adds an insurance policy – around £250 on an £800 product – unless you can prove you have home contents insurance.

Helen moved back to Barnsley to be nearer her family after splitting up with her partner. She went to BrightHouse for an Xbox (total cost about £585, but only about £200 in shops), a TV (total cost £1,800, but only about £800 in Tesco or Asda) and a freezer (total cost £1,500 versus £800 from another retailer).

'I mean you have got to do it,' she shrugs. 'You have just got to do it to live. It's my son, really. It's him going to school and not having the stuff the other kids have. When he gets an invitation to a birthday party I panic. It's going to cost me five, ten pounds. If I give a worse present than the other mums, it's like they all notice. Maybe they don't notice, but it feels like they do. And then what do I do when it's his birthday? They can't all come here, they can't see this . . .' She gestures around her tiny flat.

'Sometimes it feels like it's . . . they are taking advantage because they know you are in a situation.'

She pauses for a while and looks out of the window, then gives a short laugh. 'I don't know why you're writing this – it's just depressing. They teach them more about kids in Africa than what it's like for some people here.'

And so this is how our high street grows. Curry's is shutting down stores but BrightHouse has 200 locations across the UK and is opening more all the time. The locations are carefully selected – more than a dozen in Greater Manchester, for instance – and it announced plans to open two more in Chester and Fleetwood as part of thirty new stores declared at its results meeting in May 2011.

Those results were pretty impressive – a 16 per cent rise in annual revenues, up from £170.6 million to £197.3 million. Like-for-like turnover grew 10.7 per cent. The company's chief executive, Leo McKee, said BrightHouse, which currently employs 2,400 staff, has the potential to grow into a 650-strong chain: 'There continues to be great demand for our proposition and the company's growth prospects are good,' he told investors. This must be cheerful news for the New York hedge fund Vision Capital, which owns a majority stake in the firm. And Vision Capital probably likes cheerful news, having recently been the subject of Wall Street's Securities Exchange Commission investigation over insider trading.

'I can think of no better marker of social deprivation

than having a BrightHouse store open in your area,' says Dr Karl Dyson, specialist in community finance and affordable credit at Salford University.

'When you are serving this market there will be criticism,' McKee admitted in an interview in the *Daily Telegraph* in 2010. 'Our market is the credit-impaired with an average household income of £20,000 or less. We give those individuals access to quality products which are aspirational.' He clearly felt the journalist was of a similar class to himself, adding, 'Where you and I have the car, the foreign holiday, the kids in the good school; for my customers the aspiration is the television and the sofa.'

The Consumer Action Group (CAG) – which you could describe as the militant wing of consumer protest – issues panicking BrightHouse customers with essential legal advice sheets that underline the company's dubious tactics:

> When you enter into an agreement with BrightHouse, you are entering into a hire purchase agreement . . . When you have made all the payments on your agreement, you may (in writing – and within a 30 day period) exercise the option to have title (ownership) of the goods transferred to you. If you choose not to exercise this option, you can simply return the goods, and receive a discount (based on their current re-sale value)

towards a new Hire Purchase agreement with BrightHouse.

However, even though the goods belong to BrightHouse at all times, this does NOT mean they can just stroll into your home and remove them if you get into payment difficulties. Unless you have actually consented to their removal, BrightHouse cannot legally remove (re-possess) them until they have:

a) *Issued you with a default notice (in writing)*
b) *Given you an opportunity to put matters right (at least 14 days)*
c) *Applied for (and been granted) a court order*

These issues will be explained in more detail in a moment, but it is important to remember that: AT NO TIME CAN ANY EMPLOYEE (OR AGENT) OF BRIGHTHOUSE FORCIBLY ENTER YOUR HOME.

Strangely, and with complete disregard to guidelines from the Office of Fair Trading (OFT), BrightHouse seem to have an active policy of forcing you into further arrears and debt should you fall behind on your agreement. They will refuse to accept part-payments, and will not allow you to reduce any arrears by paying a little extra for a few weeks. Plus, to make matters worse, they will then require the FOLLOWING week's/ month's payment as well, making it even harder to 'catch up' and bring your account up to date. You will also incur a weekly 'penalty charge' (currently £2.70 per agreement).

For example, let's say your weekly payment is £25.00 (3 typical agreements – fridge, washing machine and TV), the punishment for being just ONE DAY LATE will be a required payment of £58.10. Eight days late and it becomes a staggering £91.20.

It won't be long before BrightHouse start chasing you for payment. You can expect a telephone call if your payment is just one day late! BrightHouse have also been known to phone around the names you have given as references and turn up unannounced at your home. They will bombard you with all sorts of 'threats' ranging from insisting on a set time to pay – to instant repossession, but you should simply ignore and disregard anything BrightHouse tell you unless it is in writing. Any kind of aggression or con- frontation should be avoided at all times.

If you have paid more than one third of your agreement total, BrightHouse must seek a court order before they can re-posses their goods – which are now considered as 'protected goods'. (Note – if, after one third of the agreement total has been paid and BrightHouse do re-possess their goods <u>without a court order</u> and <u>without your permission</u>, then BrightHouse are in breach of their agreement and you are entitled to claim back all payments made previously on it.)

It is worth noting that BrightHouse frequently supply second hand goods. Of course, they prefer to describe them as 'quality refurbished', but the bottom line is they will be used, re-possessed or repaired products – often up to 3 years old.

'During our research, we frequently encountered contempt and rudeness from all sections of BrightHouse,' according to the Geordie CAG advisor to whom I spoke, who first came across BrightHouse when he was made redundant two years ago. 'From till staff, to store and regional managers, through to customer service advisors and senior managers. Questions were evaded, or we were lied to. Phone calls were never returned. Emails were ignored. Problems were disregarded, and any pleas for help with arrears or payment difficulties were met with a total lack of sympathy and steadfast refusal. But all of this is hidden behind a very polished corporate image, backed up by carefully chosen high-profile charity causes, and very slick cross-media advertising campaigns.'

Since sponsoring *Home and Away* on Channel 5, however, the CAG believes BrightHouse is cleaning up its act. The ire of groups such as Church Action On Poverty, has turned towards BrightHouse's rival, Buy As You View (BAYV). Established in 1972 in South Wales, BAYV offers a coin-meter payment system. If you buy a television, the coin-meter is attached to the TV power supply. You slot a coin in to watch the telly and, at the end of a fortnight, BAYV send someone round to empty the meter.

Kathryn took a telly that should cost £900 but when her statement arrived she found she was going to pay £2,173.08. The letter BAYV sent her – on 10 April 2011 – laid out her debt in stark detail:

Amount of credit for goods: £1,301.35
Total charge for credit: £871.73
Total amount payable: £2.173.08
Opening balance: £2.173.08
Interest rate: 22.30% per annum

'I was only told four months into paying that I had insurance which I never asked for or was told about,' she explains. 'The area manger told me they did not have to tell me about the insurance. I asked the area manager for a copy of the signed credit agreement over three months ago and I have had nothing off him. He insists it will be in the office somewhere but still has not produced it. At one point I even refused to pay and I was told that if I didn't then they would send the police – as I had stolen the goods. I am in a bit of a mess over it all – I don't want to break the law but I don't see why I should pay an amount I was not aware of.'

Threatening Kathryn with the police goes beyond unethical and into menacing. But threatening customers with the police seems to be a Buy As You View tactic. In April 2011 for instance, Chris – who lives in Sunderland and had been a BAYV customer for roughly a year with monthly payments of £75 – decided to buy a new table and chairs from the company. The salesperson on the phone told him that the new purchase could be rolled up with his old agreement and refinanced over three years so that all together his payments would stay the same. With a new baby on the way, this was what he needed.

The first time payment was due, BAYV stuck to the agreement. The second time – six weeks later – the company rep came to Chris's door and demanded £105. Although his contract said he was only due £75, he stumped up the £105 'to get the guy out of my home'. He complained to BAYV who told him, reassuringly, that someone would be in touch. That day his girlfriend's pregnancy developed complications. The couple spent a few days dashing in and out of the hospital as doctors battled to save their baby. Their absence clearly incensed the BAYV rep, Paul, who scrawled a chilling note at the bottom of the company's standard You Missed Our Call Today form: 'Urgent. Last chance,' it says in biro. 'I will give you till 12 today to either return goods or pay cash, then police will come.'

On 14 June 2011, a new BAYV rep showed up on his doorstep. Chris said he was disputing the £105 payment and asked the man to show him any contract which specified he had to pay that amount. Within minutes his regular rep was at the door, saying they'd call the next day with the police. Chris asked them to bring any paperwork that proves he has to pay £105.

'The next day the same collectors turned up, this time with three police officers,' Chris said, still clearly amazed at his treatment. 'He showed me a delivery note with my girlfriend's signature basically agreeing that table was delivered to my address. I told him I wanted to see the contract, but he said, "I've come to remove your goods." I said he wasn't coming in, and as I said that one police officer said: "What did you say?" I repeated it and he arrested me for breach of the peace – on my own doorstep – handcuffed me and put me in the back of a police van then allowed the guys into my home to remove the goods.'

BAYV tried to get Chris to sign a consent form whilst he was handcuffed, which he refused, showing more confidence than I would in the same situation – in the back of a police van surrounded by three cops and two repo men – then the collectors left with his goods 'while the police de-arrested me and let me back in'.

What sort of relationship do you have with law and order if the state illegally detains you so that a private company can enter your home without a court order and repossess your telly – after unilaterally changing an agreed contract? How do you view the police if they're acting as debt collectors for a hire purchase firm? How is it possible to feel anything but alienation and anger? The amazing part of the story is Chris's patient reaction. He channelled his complaints about the policy through the correct procedures, and – after four days – they sent someone to hear his story. When BAYV requested three cops, they turned up with less than twenty-four hours' notice to help an illegal entry. When the illegal entry was reported, it took four days for the police to respond.

The BrightHouse store in Barnsley is pretty much bang in the centre of busy, pedestrianized Market Street – it's grey fascia and orange logo lurk at the base of the newish, brick-fronted building. Blue signs in the window offer no-hassle credit, low weekly payments and no deposit. Over the road and three doors up there's the South Yorkshire Credit Union – a financial cooperative owned and controlled by its members. It lends money at 1 to 2 per cent per month (APR's of 12.5 to 26.8 per cent respectively), with life insurance built in, for up to five years unsecured or ten years secured.

The South Yorkshire Credit Union was formed in 2008 with the merger of the Barnsley Credit Union, the

Dearne Valley Credit Union and the Darnum Credit Union. It is run by Ian Guest, a big, garrulous former steelworker with a gossipy tone who's patient with fools that don't understand finance. Like me. The union has a deal with the Co-operative and with Argos to supply TV sets and white goods at interest rates that massively undercut BrightHouse. The exact same 46-inch LED Samsung TV that through BrightHouse could cost over £3,000 costs £729.99 from the Co-operative, which – if bought through a credit union – costs a maximum of 2 per cent a month in interest.

The credit unions are stepping into the voids left by high-street banks in a bid to keep the poor away from sharks, marked-up goods and doorstep lenders. If the banks had felt any sense of social duty after that £850 billion bailout, they might have considered putting a cashpoint machine in deprived areas. Other companies do – but they charge £1.50 or £2 to withdraw money. Given the largest amount these machines offer is usually £40, that's a hefty percentage they're creaming off. The Royal Bank of Scotland (£20 billion of tax payers' money), Halifax/Bank of Scotland (£13 billion of tax payers' money) or Lloyds (£4 billion of tax payers' money) could install machines that only charge 50p and they'd still be helping low-income families – the £1 saved would pay for four pints of milk at Lidl or Iceland.

The credit unions don't offer ATMs – regulations don't allow it – but their main saving for members is the price of borrowing money. 'A £500 loan over 58 weeks earns the union £75,' Guest explains, sitting in a high, pillared meeting room that used to be a flashy restaurant but now houses the credit union and a couple of similar socially minded enterprises. It's got a certain mercantile grandeur to it, which might have annoyed Orwell. Barnsley came in for a drubbing in *The Road to Wigan Pier* as the council was building an expensive new town hall when he passed through and he thought the money should have gone to unemployed miners.

These days, of course, all miners in the area are ex-miners. Barnsley used to thrive on pits and clothes – clothing manufacturer S.R. Gent's sewing factory was set up over sixty years ago in the town. The last pit – in Golthorpe – closed in 1994. Marks and Spencer – which once made a point of selling British-sourced clothes – started outsourcing in 1998, cutting half S.R. Gent's workforce and starting a downward spiral that ended in administration in 2005. As a result, the union is busiest on benefit and pension days. Mondays, Tuesdays and Wednesdays have the biggest queues. Friday's tend to be wages day when people come in to take their pay from their account. The credit union offers the equivalent to a bank account to the kind of people who the banks reject – usually agency workers, who are the first out of work and the last in.

Agency work is transient – Alan, a building-site labourer who uses the South Yorkshire Credit Union, sometimes only gets one, two or three days' work a week. One week he's in Scotland, the next in a field in Lincolnshire. He never knows when he's going to work. He can't sign on as he doesn't know what hours he will be working. But he's trying.

'The people I work with want to work, even though they don't know where they're getting the work from,' he explains. 'Sometimes we have to pay our own travel, we have to pay for everything.' There are some dubious practices with the agencies about how they pay people, too. One agency only paid people through its own cash machine – a bit like an ATM – and it costs to withdraw the money. Others paid workers by cheque and then offered to cash the cheque for them.

Alice – an agency nurse looking after the elderly in residential homes – was at the union to borrow £500 to cover a shortfall because her shifts were becoming too intermittent. She'd had to break into the last of her savings in order to pay the rent, buy food and fill the car with petrol.

'The work is very short notice, usually with only an hour to get to the home, which often involves a drive of over thirty to forty miles,' she explained. 'I sometimes get dressed in my uniform and sit in the front room all ready just in case a call comes in. Of course, on the day a call doesn't come in, which is most of them, I get no pay. A lot of residential homes are in a state of crisis at present. They're understaffed but they either won't or aren't willing to afford to employ the agency staff to bring them up to strength. So on the days I do get called in, the shift will be a nightmare.'

On top of all that, the redundancy of one of the supervisors at her agency's office back in March 2011 meant that wages were a mess – she was owed, she said, around 150 hours of pay and hundreds of miles of expenses but no one seemed to have the paperwork to prove this, even though she'd sent it in.

One man, who refused to give his name, said he was at the credit union to get a loan because his cooker blew up – 'otherwise I'd have a house with three children and no food. Around here the loan sharks are pretty bad and their interest rates are crazy. It can break you.'

Guest will lend up to three times the amount you've got saved at 1 per cent interest but also offers loans to non-members, usually at a time of great crisis. 'We give loans with advice,' he explains. 'So if someone comes in and says, "I've got the bailiffs at the door, I need x thousand pounds!" we pick up the phone to the council and talk to the housing people. Because poor people tend to think the only way to solve a problem is to throw money at it. That's part of the cycle of debt they get themselves into.

'People say, "I've offered them £30 a week but I can't afford it." Well offer them a pound, I say. "I can't do that," they panic. So we try and educate them – let's deal with it properly, make offers you can afford . . .'

The largest amount Guest will loan out is £1,200 – but only as a bond for rent and he pays that direct to landlords. 'There's not so much social housing in Barnsley so the private sector is big,' he explains. 'Landlords want a bond, which is equal to one month's rent. They also want one month's rent in advance. And then there's an admin fee and key fee. So you've got families coming in here because they need a three-bedroom house and there's no social housing and they need £1,200 for the bond and rent up front. These people are pretty low benefit claimants and I wouldn't really want to lend them £1,200 – but if I don't, what do they do? They're either not going to get rehoused or they're going to borrow it from the loan shark or the high-cost lender.

'We know from experience that if you set people up to fail they will. People have rent arrears and they can't get out of it because they're still paying these high-cost lenders. And you're not helping them to set up a home as a home. We want to see more settled communities because we see such problems with these people who move every six months because of the lack of security of the tenure – and that's largely because landlords don't want to tie themselves into long-term contracts. The tenant thinks they're going to have to move on so they don't invest in the home or in the neighbourhood. Housing has a disproportionate effect on poor people. You get the midnight flit, where kids go to bed in one house and wake up in another. The kids don't get to build up friends in the street and sometimes have to move schools so it's very damaging to them educationally and socially.'

The credit union was set up ten years ago and now has 15,000 members – 9,000 in Barnsley and 6,000 in Doncaster. That 9,000 in Barnsley is roughly 6 per cent of the town's population. In deprived areas, that can rise to 17 per cent of the population. 'We look after their standing orders and direct debits – which a bank doesn't offer to them because they're chaotic,' he says proudly. 'We treat them like people. The problems of aspiration in Barnsley go back to the old pit culture – the piggy-bank savings bank, the weekly payslips, no need for an education because you'll be in the pit or factory come sixteen. How are the kids supposed to take education seriously if their parents never did?'

Guest is worried about the coming benefit changes. When the government changed benefit payments from weekly to fortnightly he found a lot of people struggled – 'the way they manage is Monday's money's for this, Tuesday's money's for that and Wednesday's money's for this. It's all going back to grandmothers with tins, saving money in the tea caddy . . . all these coping strategies will be undermined by universal benefit. I'm not against universal benefit as an idea – but paying it monthly . . . the direct debit system gets people into problems. If they're getting paid every four weeks then the benefit's going in on different dates each month and the direct debit might be set to pay out a couple of days later and they can't budget. Then the banks charge them excess fees for doing nowt – "I'm writing you this letter and charging you £35 for something I didn't do." People like cash. They know how much they've got and they know where it is.'

Speke Citizens Advice Bureau has similar worries and is offering people budgeting tips for the looming switch. It's a grim litany of neglect:

To convert weekly to monthly:
Multiply by 52 and then divide by 12
Example; £10 x 52 / 12 = £43.33

To convert monthly to weekly:
Multiply by 12 and then divide by 52
Example; £50 x 12 / 52 = £11.54

Remember, there is more than 4 weeks in each month so don't just multiply by 4 or divide by 4. If you switch from weekly to monthly payments and continue to pay 4 weeks per month, you will end up in arrears at the end of the year.

Alternatively, if you pay a quarter of your monthly bill each week, you will end up paying too much to your creditor.

Try not to lose track of these payments and don't be tempted into thinking you can fall behind because you have plenty of time to catch up.

Catching up with the payments, often leads to missing payments on other bills.

Jim pays £480 rent per month. How much does he pay per week?

Harriet spends £130 per month on her food shopping. How much does she spend per week?

Nicola pays £96.33 per quarter for her mobile phone. How much does she pay per month?

Mark pays £900 per year for his car insurance. How much does he pay per month?

Steve has booked a holiday which cost £1260.50 and has 1 year to pay for it. How much will he need to pay per week?

The switch can be vicious. In Sheffield, Ash – a single dad – lost his job as a driver for a small manufacturer and went from £400 per week wages to £420 per month benefit. Over the last two years, his gas bill has risen from £22 to £35 a week, electricity from £12 to £17 a week and the family food bill from £45 to £60 a week. There is never spare money to buy new clothes, toys or furniture. If he runs out of food for the week, there's no money left to buy extra.

He dreads school holidays – 'no free school dinners, no breakfast club,' he says, shrugging. 'They want to go to the pictures, they want to go see their mates, and they are really good kids. I've been blessed with really, really good kids. They know money is tight.' Tears appear at the corner of his eyes as he talks about them. 'They don't ask for expensive things, they never say can I have these trainers or that game. I want them to have them – I give my daughter practically all my money that I've got left, just so she can keep up. We got a grant for school uniform, new stationery and a bag and she was made up about it, it was the first new thing she'd had for years. I hope she does well at school, the love. She's always been good at science, so maybe she could go into that.'

This is heartbreaking – but it is just tourism. For all the words Ash says, it's hard to convey even a fraction of what his life is like. His street isn't bad – he's got a roof over his head. To experience it, you have to live in his house, with a slight musty smell and the tang of washing powder and stale food – not for a night or a week but for years and years.

According to the Organization for Economic Co-operation and Development (OECD), children in the UK have the lowest chance of escaping poverty out of twelve rich countries that were studied. In the UK 3.5 million children live in poverty – 1.6 million in severe poverty. Almost half the children in the UK with asthma come from the poorest 10 per cent of families. More than one million homes in the UK are currently classified as being 'unfit to live in'. These are all the deserving poor – in that they deserve better.

CHAPTER 4

Housing

As you walk through the industrial towns you lose yourself in labyrinths of little brick houses blackened by smoke . . . The interiors of these houses are always very much the same . . . All have an almost exactly similar living-room, ten or fifteen feet square, with an open kitchen range; in the larger ones there is a scullery as well, in the smaller ones the sink and copper are in the living-room. At the back there is the yard, or part of a yard shared by a number of houses, just big enough for the dustbin and the w.c.s. Not a single one has hot water laid on.

George Orwell, *The Road to Wigan Pier*, 1936

Sally lives in a tower block in Eccles, overlooking Salford precinct – the site of one of Manchester's spasms of violence in the August 2011 riots. The lifts don't work, the walls are covered in graffiti and the corridors smell of urine and smoke. Her flat has no central heating and it's freezing even in April. She's not allowed to install gas heaters, so she effectively lives in her sitting room through the winter – a long and cold season in recent years – sleeping on a sagging, velveteen sofa and huddling close to an electric heater that spins her meter like a one-armed bandit. With her TV on for a large part of the day and cooking two meals, she uses around 50 kW over twenty-four hours – roughly £5 per day, or half of her weekly benefit.

'I don't think wherever I've lived I've had central heating,' she thinks hard, shaking her head. 'I can't imagine life where I'd go in and it'd be central heated. I can't imagine what it would be like to live somewhere nice . . .' She breaks off and surveys her room. 'Look at me. It's crap. What can I say? It's crap. No heating, lots of things don't work, it's quite isolated, there's not much of a community. But you don't have a choice about where you live now.

'And it's worse even. I don't know if the government are doing it on purpose, but there's this fear that your house is not safe. There's a new rule that you have to, after two years, reapply for your council tenancy. If you get in a better position you might be asked to move. It's "Do I get a job and lose my house?" It worries me, thinking, "Where will I go? Where will I end up? What will happen to me? Have I got priority? What is priority? Has it changed again?" The whole of that . . . I don't even know how to know what the rules are. The advice service you can go to about where you can get help has stopped. Salvation Army, that's closing in town. There's just . . . what was once there as a kind of safety net is now gone. It's just gone. If you're homeless and on your arse, that's it, you're just there, deal with it.'

Salford's housing is not of the best stock. According to the 2001 census, there were still 277 homes in the area without a toilet and 6,653 without central heating. The Brookhouse Estate and the Winton Estate have particularly bad reputations. Once when a friend of mine living in east London reported gunshots to the police, they asked, gently, 'Are you sure they're gunshots, madam?' – but when she replied, 'I'm from Salford,' they had an armed response team there in three minutes. All the same, Orwell saw worse.

'When you walk through the smoke-dim slums of Manchester you think that nothing is needed except to tear down these abominations and build decent houses in their place,' Orwell wrote. 'On balance, the Corporation Estates are better than the slums; but only by a small margin.' His Manchester was noisy, smoky and crowded, showered in soot and grime, with miles of two-up two-down terraces, families crammed into rooms, outside toilets – the classic slum. These days (mostly) the toilets are inside and the water runs hot and cold if you pay your bills, but there's still poverty and misery everywhere when retracing the Road.

Amanda lives on the Bideford Estate in Baguley, Manchester, on the eleventh floor of a high rise, with two lifts that keep breaking down. She struggles with one flight of stairs, let alone eleven. The flat itself is not too bad but the neighbourhood scares her. 'There's a lot of drinkers and drug addicts there, that are literally sitting outside all day and every day,' she explains. 'You meet them in the lifts, and . . . oh, it's terrible. And some of them are not so nice either, quite rude to you, you know . . . sexually. I don't like it. I don't feel like . . . in that flat I don't feel safe.'

Nearby I met one man – white, early fifties, single – who was gradually saving to buy furniture for his council flat. He'd amassed enough cash for either a cheap single bed or a small TV and opted for the latter. He was on powerful antidepressants that sometimes made him lethargic so he'd spend days lying on the carpeted floor just watching the telly. He grouched about asylum seekers and immigrants, but halfway through the conversation, he sounded almost jealous. 'They all look after each other,' he sighed. 'They're always in each other's houses, moving in to the same streets together. I've got a son and an ex-partner and they don't even visit me. It's just me.'

There's a grim irony in the housing desolation of

northern cities – indeed, of all cities. In a way, you could say that Orwell was partly to blame. The terrible slums, the two-up two-down houses with outside toilets that he described so powerfully, were clearly untenable. People could not be expected to live in such grim conditions. And so, with the best will in the world, with everyone's best interests at heart, and driving forward to meet the technological promise of the twentieth century, architects, politicians, economists and social planners created something new – the modern housing estate.

According to Ben Bolgar, director of design at the Prince's Foundation for the Built Environment – Prince Charles's urban architecture charity – this solution wasn't only unnecessary, it was also responsible for the destruction of communities and helped spread an urban blight more socially entrenched than the dirt and chaos it was supposed to erase.

'The thing about the two-up two-down is that it's very adaptable – it's low tech, a simple design, you can knock rooms together to make it bigger, connect houses even,' explains Bolgar, an amiable man with an unruly shock of strawberry-blond hair, when we speak over the summer. 'It's been around in cities for the best part of 200 years for a reason.'

'But the modernist movement – led by the likes of Le Corbusier – despised the idea of streets. Though sociable, they had become chaotic and dirty. They had become symbols of all that was bad about the city. So modernism was about open spaces, finding clean air, bringing nature into the city. They took a row of terraced houses and turned it up on its end.

'The street became a private space – the stairs or the lifts. The residential blocks were surrounded by gardens and parks, lots of fresh air. They separated pedestrians from traffic with skywalks and long corridors serving the apartments. Some of it feels slightly sinister – in the US there really was an intention to ghettoize low-income communities. The UK had better intentions but equally poor results.'

Reformers planning social housing – from Victorian philanthropists such as George Peabody to the social housing projects of the 1960s and 1970s – wanted to solve problems. Build it green, build it near a factory, remove temptation and all would be well. With these houses, I thee mend. Some estates were built without pubs by social reformers, making it hard to meet your neighbours. You had to delouse and prove your worth – be one of the deserving poor. Even the design of houses – kitchens at the front so housewives could watch their children – carried ideas of the right sort of behaviour.

The reality of the modernist dream was far from utopian, however. The miles of corridors became mayhem for crime. They were like rabbit warrens. People could rob you, run, turn two corners and they were gone. At least on the street there was a chance that someone saw your attacker. In the sky, no one gave chase. Water ate away at prefabricated, panelized systems built quickly and cheaply, attached with insufficient bolts. The more complicated a building, the harder it is to identify the source of a leak. Lots of estates had flat roofs. On a complex estate this could mean that water could run anywhere. It was a nightmare finding the source. Buildings weathered badly and looked worse the older they got – it made people feel ill. And the green spaces did more harm than good.

'With tower blocks with large green spaces, there is less clarity about who owns the green spaces, they don't get used and people don't feel like they own them,' Bolgar explains. 'It's what we call the refrigerator theory. If you have to pay the council £30 to take your broken-down refrigerator to the dump and you don't have a car yourself where will you dump it? Streets are self-policing. If someone dumps a fridge outside your house you stop them. If they dump it at the edge of a nebulous, unbordered green space that no one feels they own and no one maintains – not even the council – then you tend not to intervene.'

Even a pleasant garden suburb, if socially engineered, has a history of ruining lives. With a house very close to the street, for instance, there's very little – other than not painting the window or doors – that you can do to affect the appearance of the street or your house. It may be anarchy out the back, but the appearance of the street is OK. Of course, this doesn't produce egalitarian perfection. All the same, it's far easier to wreck the mood of an entire neighbourhood if you have a front garden.

In the post-war housing estates that were modelled on a garden suburb with largish front gardens – such as Platt Bridge in Wigan – someone putting scrappy kids' toys or a broken-down car in the front garden can have a hugely negative impact on the area. The people in the neighbourhood might not behave that badly but it looks like they do – and people value how an area looks when estimating its value or attractiveness to live in. If a high street is full of boarded-up shops, you are less likely to wander down and browse than if it's bursting with life.

Barbara Nettleton is sixty-three. She lives on Darlington Street East, Wigan – effectively the same road Orwell stayed on when he first arrived in the town. He slept above the tripe shop at 22 Darlington Street – about half a mile down the gently sloping hill towards Wigan North Western station. Number 22 has gone – the entire terrace has gone, grassed over with a square block marking the site: 'George Orwell slept here.' Today, the interlinking network of streets, terraced houses and shops has been replaced. Darlington Street – which runs through Scholes – is now a wide dual carriageway. Opposite the strip of grass where the terraces used to be is a large branch of Lidl.

'Scholes and Ince used to be packed terraces, lots of houses, lots of pubs, lots of businesses,' Barbara remembers. 'People kept books at the shop, paid up at the end of the week. It was trusting, nice, friendly. After the war, they built Platt Bridge estate and moved all the people over from Ince. People didn't want to move but they had no choice. They didn't move neighbours together. All the people you'd lived next door to were miles away. My mum moved from a house with no central heating – we used to get frost on the glass on the window, although we were always healthy – to a house with central heating in Platt Bridge. The central heating was installed by a German company and it gradually broke down. They couldn't get the parts to get it fixed. People started moving out so the council started moving other people in, families from Liverpool, disrupting things.'

By the time the journalist Beatrix Campbell visited in 1981, she found squalid conditions with families struggling to pay huge overheads – heating bills for one and two bedroom maisonettes were £200 to £250 per quarter. Today, with soaring fuel inflation, the same struggle is looming this winter – with the winter fuel allowance for pensioners cut just before Christmas 2011. For the over 60s, it went down by £50 to £200.

For the over 80s, it was reduced by £100 to £300.

Platt Bridge is perched on a hillside, a maze-like sprawl of scruffy low-rise houses built around cul-de-sacs and dead-end lanes. You have to walk past the McDonald's drive-thru to enter the estate – the neon yellow of the giant golden m towering above all. Some of the houses are in the same state of disrepair as Campbell found – some have doors hanging from hinges, there are sheets hanging in windows, the odd graffiti tag. But the residents association is trying to repair and rebuild local playgrounds and – on royal wedding day – there were three small street celebrations dotted amidst the desolate concrete sprawl. Kids jumped on a bouncy castle and the smell of a barbecue drifted across the street near the Children's Centre.

Watching them bounce joyfully – enjoying the sun, the crowd, the day off school – it broke your heart to think how grimly the odds were stacked against them. According to research from Wigan Council, over 30 per cent of kids on the Platt Bridge estate live in poverty. They have a low chance of being breastfed, a high chance of being arrested in their teens and a very high chance of it being for drugs or violence. It's hard to imagine how the estate was sold to the miners and factory workers of Ince – here, we're moving you high on this hill. There's only one access road and you're a long way from town; you won't live near your neighbours but you will have central heating.

The nearby Scholes estate, Platt Lane, was lovely when it was first built, Barbara explains. 'It had a section for over fifties, with maisonettes and nice flats. Lots of nice people moved in. Over the years the council started moving anyone in, anyone with a criminal record, anyone arrested for drugs. Now there's a square, Innes Square, that they call Loony Square. The only time the council cleaned the place up was after the man who ran the local Chinese takeaway was murdered and the national press turned up. Then they swept the streets three times a week.'

Barbara runs a community centre, Sunshine House, on Scholes Precinct – a grim-looking 1970s square with half of the shops boarded up.

'We lost the precinct when the post office closed,' she says sadly. 'It was a domino effect. We had a paper shop, a butcher's, a fruit and veg shop, and a hairdresser. The post office used to have a queue outside on pension morning. There was no need for people to go into Wigan. But as soon as the post office closed, they had to go into town to get their pensions and benefits, so they'd buy their shopping there too. That tipped the balance. They don't understand the effect if you take something like that away. It's been a slow decline over three years. That Christmas we all got a postcard from the Royal Mail and I got everyone to send cards back to them as protest. It didn't get us the shops back though. Now the kids just gather there after dark and it makes people nervous.'

Both political parties are to blame – the Conservative governments of the 1950s and mid-1970s built more high-rise blocks than intervening Labour administrations. The last Labour government, however, engaged in slum clearance on a massive scale – part of a huge project called the Housing Market Renewal Pathfinder Programme that saw development around airports as the best way to secure London's role as the financial hub of Europe and beat off the threat of an emerging and powerful Frankfurt. The idea, as part of the constant, grinding post-war destruction of industry and fetishization of the City, was to knock down 250,000 houses in the north and build one million houses in the south – or, as the government's progress report in 2007 put it: 'the plans to tackle low demand in the north of England were set alongside measures to develop a series of growth areas in the Midlands and South'. Massive social engineering is still something the government feels entitled to toy with, despite the miserable failure of previous attempts.

Again, you can see that they meant well. The places targeted for the Pathfinder Programme had generally low house prices, quite a few empty houses, and there was a slow drift of people out of the area – although this was based on data from the 1991 census and, in many places, was out of date. The list of Pathfinder projects reads like Orwell's route map: Birmingham, Staffordshire, Manchester, Merseyside, South Yorkshire,

Hull, Newcastle, Oldham and East Lancashire. Each was given a funky new name – Liverpool was New Heartlands, Birmingham was Urban Living, Oldham was Partners in Action whilst Nelson fell under Elevate East Lancashire.

The idea of regenerating these areas sounds so positive, although the gentrification of Sheffield's infamous Park Hill estate – the brutalist flats that tower over the station that are usually the first thing you see as you arrive in the city – was described by Owen Hatherley, author of *Militant Modernism: A Guide to the New Ruins of Great Britain*, as 'class cleansing'.

Park Hill estate grew out of the city's slum clearance and building began in 1957 with the aim of building 1,900 flats for Sheffield's poor. The estate was finished in 1961. The first settlers were thrilled with their self-contained world.

'My gran loved Park Hill,' explains Graham, who moved off the estate in the late 1980s – although his gran refused to go and still lives nearby in a residential care home, within sight of the concrete behemoth. 'It was convenient for town and the markets. There was recreation built in with the bingo in the complex's social centre and there were the four pubs also on the complex. Everything was warm and modern, great new facilities – a world away from tin baths, outside loos and back-to-back slums. Because many of the people moved into the flats all came from the same small area, at the time of opening the sense of community and community responsibility was nurtured. The choice of shops at the time on the complex was fantastic, and with the waste-disposal Garchey system, which was so innovative it meant you didn't have hassle disposing of garbage, it was hi-tech living, after a fashion.'

Park Hill's wide, airy walkways proved a problem. They were as open-ended and tricky to police as the Victorian terraces they replaced, so the project decayed from a source of intense municipal pride to dilapidated sink estate. 'Park Hill is commonly described as the "largest listed building in Europe" or the largest listed 60s building,' Hatherley argues. 'In fact both those titles belong to London's Barbican Estate: a place that, like Park Hill, is full of bare concrete, open space, urban density, walkways, social facilities – both contain several schools and pubs, although only one an arts centre – and the separation of pedestrian and car. One is a problem that apparently had to be solved; the other is one of London's most prestigious addresses.'

One, of course, has always been cleaned and cared for, the other left alone to decay. Towards the end of the last Labour government, with the assistance of public money from English Heritage and the Homes and Communities Agency, a property developer started rebuilding Park hill, moving the residents out to other towns or estates at the edge of the city.

'It's all a microcosm of how public housing was

treated during the boom,' Hatherley argues. 'Property speculators became hungry for previously neglected spaces, going from regenerating derelict factories all the way to redeveloping dilapidated council estates. But in the latter case, there were people in the way, who first had to be decanted, or evicted as it used to be called, albeit with the promise of a "right of return". Yet already more former Park Hill tenants have registered their interest in returning than there will be social units to accommodate them.'

Over in Nelson, East Lancashire – which fell under the Elevate Pathfinder Programme – regeneration almost caused riots. One of the six wards targeted by Elevate was Whitefield, centred on Every Street, a busy shopping area sandwiched between the M65 and the railway line. Nelson is an old millworkers' area famous for industrial unrest between the wars – it was nicknamed Little Moscow and refused to celebrate King George V's silver jubilee in 1935.

The Asian community in Every Street and the surrounding network of two-up two-downs had been displaced twice by the time the local authority bought up the end of the street and boarded it up in 2002 – as part of an earlier regeneration decision that was subsumed into the grand Pathfinder Plan.

Ostensibly the community was consulted. At the time of writing, a report from the planners, Nathaniel Lichfield & Partners, is still online and makes for instructive reading. Having decided to regenerate, the council had three options: renew old housing (patch and mend), knock down some decrepit old housing and renew the rest (thinning) or comprehensive redevelopment.

To find out what the residents thought, the council held six workshops – one in each ward. At the meetings, as the report states, all wards backed a combination of patch and mend and thinning. Every part of the town listed – without prompting – roughly the same desires for their area: clean the place up and plant a few trees, more police patrols, more traffic calming/ speed cameras, some sports or community facilities especially for the young, and some good local jobs.

The report concludes:

The issues flowing from the initial consultation in response to the strategic options suggested that at this stage in the process there was an acknowledgement among most residents in the town that there is a problem of housing market failure to be tackled. However, there was less consensus as to the drivers of this problem and of the scale and type of change that might be needed. Part of this derived from an apparent scepticism of change, and of the ability of local agencies to deliver it, but also from the understandable difficulty for some residents to contemplate radical change without more information on its practical implications and what it might mean on the ground and for their circumstances.

And so Nathaniel Lichfield & Partners came up with the preferred option – the high levels of change option (preferred by almost none of the residents) that involved creating the Nelson Regeneration Arc – a sweeping change to the town centre that included knocking down 1,800 houses and old industrial buildings and building 450 new homes. Awkwardly, the planners concluded, it was hard to be sure how much of the urban blight in Whitefield was natural and how much had been caused by the council's original compulsory purchase order (CPO) as opposed to the supposed natural decline:

> The Whitefield area has difficulties and problems of empty houses. The reasons for this are complex, but do include the results of the blight caused by the CPO. The challenge, however, is what to do with the empty properties now, and to make a judgment as to how far it is possible to secure re-occupating given the housing market, and to secure investment in bringing retained properties back into use, including those that are the smallest and least popular housing types. There are no easy

answers here, and plenty of risk involved in whatever option is taken forward.

In other words: it was the council's fault, but all the same, best to carry on. It became a designed blight. House prices fell from £20,000 to £7,000. Then, for reasons no one in the community understood, a large fence was thrown up around one of the buildings – like a construction site. The council got permission to close the road. There was such bad feeling about having the street closed down that community leaders worried a riot would break out.

Every Street was a very mixed community and terraced housing's adaptability suited its needs. There were families who had bought four or five houses and knocked them through so that the extended family could all live together in a seven-bedroom house. The back yards of the houses were exclusively female space; women would hang their washing and talk to their neighbours. Out the front was male territory. The two-up two-down couldn't have been more appropriate.

The mixed community fought Elevate through an unusual and vigorous alliance between the Asian and white communities, spearheaded by two strong, forth-right women – Jamila Khan and Sylvia Whitfield. They called in the Prince's Foundation for the Built Environment.

'We asked the council what their criteria were for

knocking these houses down,' Bolgar explains. 'They said due to diversifying the housing stock. We asked them to define diversity and they couldn't say. So we did a project where we took pictures of the seven bedroom houses, the five beds, the three beds, the bedsit – we did a huge map with all the different properties on, showed it to the council and said, this looks pretty diverse. We got people involved like Urban Splash who modified the little alleys that ran down the side of the houses, put the kitchens in the attic . . . it worked.'

The council lost its planning application after the women wrote to the Deputy Prime Minister's Office, but nevertheless kept up the pressure. The councillors nodded wisely at the plans from Urban Splash then appointed their own team of architects, Maccreanor Lavington, and developer R.gen.

'Even though residents preferred their [Urban Splash] plans, a scheme has got to be deliverable,' Pendle Council's regeneration manager insisted. 'It all comes down to long-term sustainability and cost.' All the same, it was a victory for the community. Only sixteen homes were demolished and seventy new ones were built.

In Nelson, they were lucky – there was a coordinated community response uniting white and Asian, Prince Charles got involved and the council saw reason. Overall, however, the Housing Market Regeneration

Pathfinder Programme steamrollered on. In Newstead, Nottinghamshire, regeneration was rushed to build premises for businesses to move into, so they built over allotments. In Highgate, in South Yorkshire's Dearne Valley, they paved over half of a playing field to build a link road.

Richard, an ex-miner turned social worker who played football for his working men's club, had played on the pitch as a schoolboy – it had a lot of memories. 'If it had been a theatre they'd paved over there would have been a huge fuss,' he argues. 'People don't see a football pitch or a playing field as having cultural value. They see it as being about fitness, and that's it. But the bit of land you used to go to after school to play football and mess about has iconic value.'

In Highgate there had been paths that cut across fields between mining towns, which got built over. The new houses blocked people's pastoral views. 'If people look out over a field they think they're living in the countryside,' Richard explains. 'If you replace that with a housing estate that looks like any other housing estate, they've lost something.'

People from Leeds and Sheffield bought up lots of the new houses in these upscale developments. Locals stretched themselves with mortgages from Northern Rock, pushing what they could afford in order to move out of their council homes – so the council estates emptied and the only people who moved in were asylum seekers. The new commuter residents socialized near work, staying in Sheffield and Leeds to spend their wages.

'The population rose by 25 per cent but the town grew quieter and quieter on Friday and Saturday nights,' Richard says. 'It may just be cars, or people who aren't involved in the community – but it died.'

The Dearne Valley has been taking it on the chin for some time. 'When they took the jobs away, about 20 per cent of the population went with them,' Richard explains. 'Lots of the miners went to work on the Channel Tunnel. They did fine. But the ones with family or with less get up and go – they stayed. The 20 per cent who left, they left empty housing stock. So they dumped the problem families there. In a village called Wetwang they kept putting antisocial families from Hull. The Hull kids in particular had a big impact. For fourteen-year-olds the bad kids are attractive role models.'

It was Richard who I spoke to on the Friday before the August 2011 riots and who made the point that people want to be respected. 'They don't like being ignored. Over the last thirty years it's been lots of little things, little jabs and cuts, that combine to make a big thing – this sense, with nothing to contradict you, that nobody cares what you say.' It was Richard who said, 'I don't know why people aren't rioting.'

Owen Hatherley agrees. 'Look at Bristol, a port where

you could walk for miles and wonder where its working class had disappeared to, which seems to have been given over completely to post-hippy tourism, "subversive" graffiti, students and shopping,' he suggests. 'Well, those invisible young, socially excluded people arrived in the shiny new Cabot Circus mall and took what they wanted, what they couldn't afford, what they'd been told time and time again they were worthless without. Look at Liverpool, where council semis rub up against the mall-without-walls of Liverpool One, whose heavy-security streets were claimed by the RIBA to have "single-handedly trans-formed Liverpool's fortunes" as if a shopping mall could replace the docks. Look at Manchester's city centre, the most complete regeneration showpiece, practically walled-off from those who exist outside the ring-road. Look at Salford, where Urban Splash sells terraces gutted and cleared of their working-class population, to MediaCity employees with the slogan "own your own Coronation Street home". This is urban Britain, and though the cuts have made it worse, the damage was done long before.'

In most places the Pathfinder Programme stopped after the demolition but before the rebuilding. The urban areas and the coalfields are being returned to their rotting state. The £2.3 billion project had been due to run until 2018, but was axed by the coalition government in last year's spending review. Around thirty authorities have been left to manage the half-finished regeneration work with a one-off grant of £30 million.

It's nice to think that with a bit of community organization – as in Nelson – the project could have been steered to meet local needs. For the Dearne Valley, for instance, it was the first bit of regeneration they'd seen since the miners' strike of 1984–5.

'It was a very New Labour project combining the council, business leaders, the Coalfield Regeneration Trust – it was good-hearted, part of the good stuff that New Labour did,' Richard admits. 'The Tories left the coalfields to rot. This did at least try to develop the area, although it probably relied a bit too much on public sector money.'

We'll never know for sure how it would have turned out if it had been done properly, with community consultation, led from the bottom up giving people the things they wanted – homes, jobs, safe streets, more police and some trees.

The wreckage of the Housing Market Regeneration Pathfinder Programme is easy to find, however. Heading into Manchester's terraced streets in April 2011, in my mind I still had lingering traces of Orwell's own descriptions of housing at the heart of industrial cities. I was travelling with Herbie – something like an eco-healthy meals-on-wheels service. The two Herbie vans – driven by Pete and Al – roll through the post-industrial streets of Ancoats, Clayton, Openshaw and Beswick following bus-route-style journeys and selling affordable, fresh fruit and vegetables to residents living in areas of East Manchester with poor access to fresh foods.

It's a worthy scheme that Orwell might dismiss as *New Statesman* patronage, but Pete – who drives the larger van – is no bleeding-heart, *Guardian*-reading liberal. Pete is as hard as nails. He left school at fifteen and spent his teenage years pushing Triumph, Norton and BSA motorbikes to their limit – bombing up and down between the Ten Ten Coffee Bar, at 1010 Stockport Road, and London's Ace Cafe, all decked out in denim, leathers and a nasty forearm tattoo reading 'hate'. 'I tell people it's supposed to read Kate but my tattooist was dyslexic,' he said unconvincingly.

As we weaved through narrow streets, a huge football stadium edged ever closer until it towered over us. 'Council pitch,' Pete nodded, dismissively. 'Left over from the Olympic games bid. No one wins anything on that.'

I did a double take. Council pitch? It did have City of Manchester stadium on the side which . . . 'Um, isn't that Manchester City's ground?' I ventured.

Pete gave me a withering glance. 'You mean you couldn't tell I'm a Red Devil?' he sighed. 'You're going to have to pay a bit more attention, Stephen.'

Staring out of the window, the strangest thing I saw was how desolate and empty the streets are now. We would drive for minutes without seeing anyone, weaving in and out of alternating back-to-back *Coronation Street*-style houses – indeed, we drove along Coronation Street itself, which connects Greer Street to Victoria Street in a matriarchal triangle. Instead of dirty, closely packed housing there were acres and acres of desolate ground all grassed over. You could still see the outline of streets, see where rows of houses used to be – but now, nothing. It was as if the Triffids had arrived.

Along Toxteth Street, hundreds of houses looked to have been demolished – the razed ground was fenced off in serried rows of desolation, entirely free of builders, developers, earth-moving equipment or scaffolding until we reached the final few side roads, where one slow-moving JCB was spreading thick soil across barren lots. One or two lots further off were already sprouting grass. It looked as if they were bulldozing homes to create parkland – an insane idea. And yet, by the K Café where we met and lunched, there were three large, flat, grassy parks that used to be houses too. Pete pointed out a wooden sign saying 'redevelopment opportunity'.

We drove down Ben Street, another row of back-to-backs, on our way to visit Marge, an elderly regular customer for Pete's fresh fruit and veg. Almost every house on her side of the road was boarded up, with thick metal grilles over the doors and windows. Marge seemed grateful to see Pete. She tottered out of the house and struggled with the high step at the side door of the large van. Her dress looked dirty, and she stared around as if slightly dazzled by daylight.

'You OK?' Pete asked.

'Not so bad . . .'

'Why are all the houses boarded up?' I asked her.

She looked at me for half a second, and then gave a faint smile. 'Son, it's been like this for ten years.' Her voice had surprising strength and power. 'There's only me and my neighbour on this side of the road. Next door left, that wasn't too long ago.' She indicated a grille across the door beside us. 'Now the kids have already stripped the roof of lead. You could have moved someone in six months ago. Northern Counties say they're redeveloping, refurbishing, but they've not really told us what's been going on. Now there's all the cutbacks. Sometimes they move people in for a while then back out again. I don't really know.'

She turned back to Pete and paid for her fruit and veg: five bananas, six potatoes for baking – 'one for each day' – and a handful of carrots. It came to 70p. She only had 60p so Pete let her off the other 10p. 'You owe me though,' he warned her. 'Don't leave the country. Although if you can work out how to leave the country on 10p let me know.'

She trundled slowly back through her front door,

leaving the street deserted. The metal grille covering the windows on the property next door was painted white with a George Cross hastily daubed across it in scarlet. 'England', it said on the sill, probably left over from the world cup. Although it didn't look like England loved Ben Street in return. We were the only people on the street. The entire place looked abandoned.

'What is there to come out of your house for?' Pete asked rhetorically as we stared at the empty tarmac. 'There's nothing to do, nowhere to go. There are no shops, the pubs have all shut. All you've got is a giant Morrisons. When I was growing up round here, every street in Clayton you used to see hopscotch or lads playing kinga – knocking on doors and running away. Now you don't see anybody playing.'

After Herbie's delivery round, we rolled down Old Ashton Road, taking in lines of new developments, all empty. I asked for whom they were intended. 'You go in the pubs and everyone's saying they're giving them away to people on the dole or asylum seekers, which is bollocks,' he snorts. 'It's like these pubs that are full of benefit cheats at dinner time. There are no pubs like that because the pubs have all closed round here. It's just what gets people angry so they pass it on and hate a bit more.'

Herbie is struggling to find funding. The National Lottery has asked them to come up with a profitable business plan that would mean they raised their prices and sold in wealthier areas – which is the exact opposite of the idea of good, cheap, healthy food for poorer people upon which Herbie was founded. 'We've got some funding problems and we've thought about asking Manchester United for money to keep going,' Pete said. 'I mean, they got paid £80 million for Ronaldo. No one's worth that. I mean, Rooney's on £250,000 a week. Mind you, he's a Scouser. I can't see him being made up about feeding Mancs.'

Fellow feeling or not, the streets looked the same in Toxteth as in Toxteth Street when I went to Liverpool a few weeks later. Street after street in the infamous L8 district – the only place in mainland Britain where the police have ever used tear gas, fired off during nine days of rioting in 1981 – was grassed over. Shops were closed, pubs boarded up. The terraced street where Ringo Starr was born is next to face the bulldozer with nothing planned in its place. It's like a scorched-earth policy or desperate firefighting, pulling down buildings to stop flames leaping across the city. The result is silent desolation.

Tullett Prebon's note to investors by Dr Tim Morgan, global head of research, outlines his headline points to resolve 'the recent social disorder': 'The consumerist ethos, in which a materialist vision is both pedalled and, for the vast majority, simultaneously ruled out by exclusion, has extremely damaging consequences, both social and economic. Britain needs to change its ethos, recast its role models, encourage saving, channel private investment into the creation rather than the inflation of assets, and switch public spending from consumption to investment within a focus on house-building, infrastructure and technology.'

This government, however, announced a budget cut for the construction of affordable homes of nearly 50 per cent from £8.4 billion to £4.5 billion in October 2010. Meanwhile, the system for managing council housing financing – the Housing Revenue Account subsidy system – is set to be replaced with an undisclosed 'self-financing' arrangement. Funding for a promised 150,000 new 'social' homes, it is proposed, could be raised by allowing housing associations to charge their tenants a new 'Affordable Rent' tenancy at 80 per cent of the market rate – significantly higher than at present.

A letter sent to the Prime Minister by Secretary of State for Communities Eric Pickles, leaked to the *Observer* in July 2011, warned, 'we could see an additional 20,000 homelessness acceptances as a result of the total benefit cap. This on top of the 20,000 additional acceptances already anticipated as a result of other changes to housing benefit.' The letter suggested that the reforms could result in fewer homes being built, as the housing benefit cap will prevent developers recouping costs through rent, giving them no incentive to build new properties. 'Initial analysis suggests that of the 56,000 new affordable rent units up to 23,000 could be lost . . . And reductions would disproportionately affect family homes rather than small flats.'

Government policy, in other words, is directing more vulnerable people towards homelessness or the private rented sector. And yet the private sector isn't working. Lisa Maria Llewellyn moved into a flat in Heaton, Newcastle, while she was heavily pregnant. As soon as she moved in, she discovered there were many, many problems with the flat. The lights didn't work. One day the window in the kitchen fell out of its frame because the wood was rotten through.

'It could have killed one of us if it hit us,' she says, horrified. 'I told the landlord – Paul – what had happened and he accused me of breaking it. After that, I had a constant flurry of harassment and abuse. He threatened me and my guarantor, sent people round to the house and then issued us with an illegal eviction notice. He took us to court because he wanted me out and imposed a £600 a day sanction. The court ruled it was an invalid notice of possession so the case was kicked out. Then he got a legal section 21 and evicted me afterwards. I'm in social housing now and would never go private again. I've lived in four private-sector places and they have all been awful.'

Kirstie Davidson, from Macclesfield, moved into her place about three years ago with her partner and six-month-old son. 'It was the first place I had ever rented so was careful to choose somewhere I felt I could really make my home. The property had been recently redecorated and painted so I was pleased with it. But almost as soon as we moved in the damp and mould started to come. Initially it was just in the corners of the rooms, but quite quickly it spread to cover the walls. We made attempts to stop it by keeping the windows open and I bought a dehumidifier, which cost a lot of money. The mould started to grow on the books on my shelves, our clothes and also the mattress in my son's cot.' She shivers. 'It was truly disgusting. I spoke to my landlord about it and her husband came over to inspect the place then said he wasn't prepared to do anything about it. For health reasons, I've decided we had to leave, but as soon as I handed my notice in I started getting abusive phone calls from the landlady.'

In July 2011, a survey by the homeless charity Shelter found that 7.5 million people in the UK have had issues with their landlord in the past ten years and some three million of them say they tried to talk to their landlord but no action was taken. Worryingly about 550,000 people said they did nothing because they were scared of the consequences.

In the last three months of 2010, courts in England and Wales dealt with 34,443 repossessions by private landlords, although the government closing 142 county courts around the UK does mean it takes longer to throw people out. Repossession claims have traditionally taken six to ten weeks, according to Sim Sekhon, director of Legal4Landlords, but the timescale is currently at three months or more thanks to a backlog of cases. 'Further delays could cost landlords thousands of pounds and enormous amounts of stress as they try to deal with unruly tenants,' he says, fretting.

To be fair, we're just beginning a sustained period of stress for tenants, too. As of November 2010, there were 4.8 million people receiving help with their rent – housing benefit or Local Housing Allowance – with 1.5 million of those renting in the private sector. At that point the maximum amount of benefit paid was set at the median average (middle value) of a sample of rents in a local area.

In Wigan, for instance, this meant someone in a one-bedroom flat could get up to £86.30 per week. In April 2011 the government switched the maximum from the median to the 30th percentile – a wall of misunderstanding for a maths dunce like me. In other words, it means giving tenants access to the bottom 30 per cent of the market instead of the bottom 50 per cent. As of January 2012 single people under the age of thirty-five are restricted to the rate for a single room in a shared house, rather than for a one-bedroom property. In Wigan, these two changes mean housing benefit tops off at £57.73 for people under thirty-five.

On the PADZ rental website in September there was

just one property available for under £100 per week in Wigan – £86 per week for a one-bedroom flat above a shop in Billinge, halfway between Wigan and St Helens and within earshot of the M6. The kitchen had a hob and oven and MDF cabinets; the bathroom had a toilet and shower of roughly the same width, jammed in side by side; the bedroom and the living room had fake parquet PVC floor covering. It's out of the range of twentysomethings looking for work, which is just as well as it's hard to get to any work from there unless you have a car. There was no property available at prices that anyone looking for work could afford.

In April 2013, the rates will be cut still further – benefit has so far increased with inflation as measured by the Consumer Price Index (CPI). Next year, it will be measured by the Retail Price Index (RPI). Both are measures of inflation, but RPI includes housing costs and mortgage interest payments while CPI does not. The switch will cut roughly £6 per week. At the same time, the government will hand housing benefit over to local councils, cutting 10 per cent from the budget. The most someone looking for their first job could afford in Manchester would be around £50 per week. At the same time, 'over occupiers' – people who live in houses with more bedrooms than they need, even if they've lived there for years – will either have to ship out or pay much higher rents.

The National Housing Federation points out that the

average social household receiving housing benefit has an annual income of just £8,320 a year. "The under occupation" penalty will leave vulnerable families with a shortfall of £676 to make up,' according to the Federation's chief executive David Orr. 'In the vast majority of cases, people will simply not be able to make up the shortfall themselves and could end up being sucked into poverty and spiralling levels of debt.'

There's an obvious conclusion to this – people, especially young people, are going to become homeless. It's already happening. In 2010, councils reported 44,160 people homeless – an increase of 10 per cent on the previous year and the first increase in almost a decade. Another 189,000 people were also placed in temporary accommodation, such as small hotels and B&Bs – a 14 per cent increase on the previous year. In August 2011 a report, written by academics from the University of York and Heriot-Watt University, Edinburgh, predicted a rise in middle-class families living on the streets and that the government's new affordable house-building regime would fall short of meeting housing targets – building fewer than 50,000 homes by 2015, which is 'well short of the 80,000 required to meet ministers' targets'.

Of course, we should pay attention if only for selfish reasons. If we have our generation of alienated youth growing up with no investment in society at all – with no bricks and mortar, no jobs, no money and no roof over their heads – it's a volatile situation. There's trouble brewing. The 1979 Tory government introduced housing benefit as Britain's manufacturing base collapsed – it eased the transition to a workless economy and avoided the unemployed rioting. Now housing benefit is being slashed as jobs vanish and available homes dry up. But more than that – what sort of country could you pledge allegiance to that wiped out a generation's hopes without apology or recompense?

Right now we're relying on charities such as Depaul to pick up the slack. The charity provides hostel accommodation for 2,000 young people aged sixteen to twenty-five. The Depaul hostel in Burnage Lane, Manchester, has suffered 35 per cent budget cuts – one hostel in Rochdale recently closed, another is threatened. Burnage is a low-support hostel – it isn't equipped to deal with addiction, disability or severe mental health issues, although sometimes the staff find themselves dealing with them anyway.

Burnage Lane houses eleven residents at a time – they can stay for up to two years, although in June the longest-serving resident had been there fifteen months. Since January 2011, ten new faces had arrived and ten old faces departed, mainly off to other supported accommodation. The theory is that they're on the list for a council house, but the waiting-list system has recently been revamped – categories used to be measured A to G, but are now 1 to 4. Homeless teenagers were up in the A bracket – in line for a flat to get their lives restarted. They've been shifted down to 4, not quite end of the line but close.

Because Burnage Lane is a low-support hostel, it's in a converted Victorian house – although it's been redecorated within the past few years and feels like a student hall of residence. There's a lounge, pool table, even a room in the basement with some weights and a punchbag . There's also a communal kitchen with a cupboard for each resident. The cupboards are always empty, however. Despite a strong sense of camaraderie – you'd often see ten kids outside passing a single cigarette between them or cooking up a meal and sharing it out with anyone passing through – it is just accepted that stuff gets stolen.

'Where they're usually coming from is children's homes,' explained the manager, Caroline – a sparky, motherly woman with an accent mixing Cheshire with traces of Ireland. 'They've got nowhere else to put them. You turn sixteen, nineteen you're out as soon as they find you a place. And when they say they're going to find you a place it's a hostel. And then the sixteen-year-old, because they've been in care that long as well, they've got this attitude – well, if I get kicked out it's okay, the social worker will take care of me and will find me somewhere to live. They're not really prepared for living in a hostel situation because they're very aggressive with staff. They've been able to get away with it in the care home, and they don't realize they can actually be punished by a warning. If they get so many warnings then eventually they will get kicked out of the project. It's really hard.'

I said that I thought it was strange that systems would be prepared to put people on the streets and give them almost no money. Didn't it seem cruel?

'That's what they actually do, though.' She was almost pleading now. 'They really do do it. When you're in a desperate situation and you need to get money there's so many barriers there to stopping you getting your money. Some of the young people at our place have been sanctioned from benefits, because they've either turned up for an interview late or didn't go to an appointment. But half of the time they haven't been told about these appointments. The benefits people are on targets that they've got to meet to get so many people off benefits per week so it's good for them to mess people about basically. So they'll get their money cut down to . . . instead of £50 a week they'll get it cut down to like £31 a week. Out of that they have to pay £10 rent and then they've got their food and then they've got, like, cigarettes . . . cigarettes might not be important but it is when you've got nothing else. It relieves stress and it helps . . . but they end up with absolutely nothing, and they're getting sanctioned every other week and it takes them about six weeks to get out. It can take six months.'

How late is late for an appointment? What sort of leeway do they give? Half an hour? I asked Caroline.

'They don't,' she was suddenly cross. 'They don't give them any leeway. There was one lad whose sick note was late so eventually he got it backdated. He was expecting his money on Saturday but it didn't arrive so he phoned the benefits up on the Monday and they said, "Well if it doesn't arrive by the Wednesday, ring us back and you'll be entitled to a crisis loan." He did that and they said, "No, you're not entitled to a crisis loan because your money might arrive in another couple of days." But in-between time he's had no money whatsoever. So he's getting into rent arrears and having to beg food.

'We try and help out as best we can, if we can we'll . . . you know, sometimes we get donations of food. At the moment we've got donations of biscuits so they're actually living on biscuits. And we do teach them to cook, you know, like try and make the best out of their money and, say, teaching them to cook soup 'cause that's cheap to make and it will last . . . but they don't think like that, young people don't think about that. It's convenient food and that's what they'll buy – big bags of twenty sausages or eight beefburgers for £1 from Iceland and microwave the lot for their evening meal. It is the worst sort of food you can eat but that's what they're eating.'

Charles – twenty-two years old, tall, white and skinny – proved her point, putting twenty fish fingers on to a plate and microwaving them at full power for a few minutes before stuffing them down. They came out steaming and shiny, looking damp and grey. He's been benefit-sanctioned since January, living on £35 per week. He had been to the Job Centre to inform them he was homeless and applied for a number of jobs whilst there. They told him he needed to check in on a job at a nearby Job Centre, but didn't say it had to be that day. The following day he found he'd been sanctioned for six months until July for missing the interview. He appealed, and the appeal date was set for 25 June.

Job Centres seem to have a nasty sense of humour. Asif has a criminal record. This disqualifies him immediately from a number of jobs – including the fire service. Last week he was sent to three interviews on three consecutive days, including one for the fire service, where the first question was . . . 'Do you have a criminal record?' End of interview. Back to the hostel.

Benefit sanctions were worse in Rochdale, Charles explained. There you'd get sanctioned for one mistake. At least in Manchester it was usually three strikes and you're out. 'But it's always the older ones who know the score,' he grinned ruefully. 'They know the scams and the forms and what you have to do. They've got mates behind the counter. It's always the younger ones or the new ones, the ones who've never signed on, who get it wrong and get the sanctions. If you're a proper benefit family, you know how to play the system.'

From his £35, the hostel took £10, leaving him £25 for everything else. When the money came through he'd head down to Iceland and stock up, but usually – as he budgeted £5 for food – it wasn't quite enough to last the week. He relied on the odd handout at meal times. The rest of the £20 had to cover bus fares, cigarettes and, most weeks, a £5 bag of weed. Clothes and toiletries didn't figure on his shopping list. 'A bit of a smoke, it's a treat,' he said, shrugging. 'It's like the relief as you smoke the first one – like, I deserve this after that week. There's only two in here who don't smoke – Andy because he's always playing football and Ayaan cos he's para.'

Ayaan was one of the current crowd who didn't seem like the supposed low-support type at all. Three residents were women fleeing forced marriages – at best abandoned, at worst pursued by their families. One kid had been living in a bus shelter for two weeks after his aunt threw him out, and was still attending college, despite having all his clothes stolen. When he finally secured a room at Depaul, his college mates had a whipround for clothes so he turned up with a bulging suitcase and a guitar, despite explaining, shamefacedly, that he didn't know how to play the guitar. Because he'd been kicked out of a family home, he'd only just applied for income support – a process that was going to take at least ten days. Until then, he was living on handouts from his friends.

Ayaan was different. The night before, there had been a row. Two residents had struck up a relationship and in the early evening the guy had attacked his girlfriend. As fists were thrown and staff tried to calm the situation, Ayaan began to panic. He's got serious mental health problems, so when he panics, it's not just shortness of breath and the fear. Caroline tried to get him to the psychiatric ward at the hospital but they said they couldn't take him in until he'd actually tried to kill himself. So they brought him back and talked him down.

We spoke in the TV room – a small lounge with chairs and a sofa. His right hand is missing – a condition he'd been born with. In rural Pakistan, where his family come from, this marked him out – although the family feud that took his father was about money rather than superstition.

'My uncles killed my dad for property and all the property came in my name,' he explained slowly. 'I have all the property and then they had to kill me to get property and my mum. So the police know my uncles and worked for them. So if they caught us they will prove that we are terrorists and we have to spend our whole life in prison and they would get all the property. I have a nice uncle, and he helped me escape. The plan was we will stay here in England for a few days. I'll come here and I'll stay for a few days and then my mum and my uncle come and then we'll go to USA from here because going to USA from Pakistan is impossible. But my mum and my uncle couldn't get in. My uncle knows I'm in Manchester. My mum knows I'm in England, she doesn't know I'm in Manchester and I am looking for her. We went to the Red Cross. I wrote to them and then they helped me to look in England and they can't find my mum and they're looking in Europe and can't find my mum.'

'Do the Red Cross know if your mum went back to Pakistan?' I asked.

'They don't know,' he said quietly. 'The Red Cross can't go into Pakistan. It makes me anxious. But people are kind and they help me. I've got nurses, psychiatrist, social worker and manager and they all help me. They took me to A&E yesterday,' he didn't pause, accepting it as one of those things, 'and then I've been discharged and two came to see me with my nurse and my nurse will come to see me on Monday as well.'

He's been in the hostel for one year and three months, and he's happy there – everyone is very friendly. He's trying to get a job, but because he only has one hand local shops have turned him down. 'The Pakistani people, they look at my hand and they say, "No, sorry, we haven't got a job."' He seems sad. 'Somebody told me all the big companies, like Asda, Sainsbury's, Lidl, they've got a specific section for disabled people. They are not allowed to employ normal people in this section. If there were two people or three people they have to employ the disabled people, is it true?'

I briefly swelled with pride that this amazed him, this act of institutional kindness. 'So would you say that you are optimistic or pessimistic? Are you hopeful or unhopeful for the future?' I asked.

'It varies, it sometimes changes,' he said. 'Now, I'm optimistic but I don't know, in half an hour, an hour I become pessimistic. I'll do a BTEC next year and then BTEC Level Two next year and then I hope university, but there was a guy, he's from England, he was born in England, and he says, "You won't go to university." I said, "Why?" He said, "Because we'll go to university, we'll get loans, for so much money, for £9,000 as well and then after university finishes we have to pay for our loan, but we're not getting jobs, so there's no point in going to university."'

'Has that put you off?'

'No. And I know how I can pay the loan back. I want to become an English player, batsman or bowler in cricket and I want India to play with us, and I'll beat them. That's what I want to do.'

I looked at him – one hand, pursued and attacked, a refugee taken in and cared for, given all the help possible, who can't quite believe there are companies that would choose to employ a disabled person, who wants to study, become an engineer and then – bless his dreams and ambitions with tears in my liberal eyes – play cricket for England and win. And I thought – that's the England I believe in. That's my lion and my unicorn.

CHAPTER 5

Unemployment

When you see the unemployment figures quoted at two millions, it is fatally easy to take this as meaning that two million people are out of work and the rest of the population is comparatively comfortable. I admit that till recently I was in the habit of doing so myself. A Labour Exchange officer told me that to get at the real number of people *living on* (not drawing) the dole, you have got to multiply the official figures by something over three. This alone brings the number of unemployed to round about six millions. But in addition there are great numbers of people who are in work but who, from a financial point of view, might equally well be unemployed, because they are not drawing anything that can be described as a living wage. Allow for these and

171

their dependants, throw in as before the old-age pensioners, the destitute and other nondescripts, and you get an *underfed* population of well over ten millions.

George Orwell, *The Road to Wigan Pier*, 1936

Adele used to work in an old people's day centre but was made redundant at the end of 2010, going from £18,000 a year to £65 a week. 'I'm actually researching frugal living. Just to . . . ways to save money, you know?' she says, pulling a thin cardigan around her as if it was cold outside.

'I went into the shop the other day and the butter had gone up 5p which has now put that out of my reach – because I can't justify spending that extra 5p when I could be doing something else with it. I never thought I'd be in a state that I'd have to do that again. I remember when my daughter was young and it was just me and her and I was so poor once the only thing I had in my house was onions. I made onion soup for us both and I had a couple of slices of bread because we had nothing else in the house. And I never thought I'd be going back to that time.'

Her rent and council tax is paid but her gas, electric and water isn't. She reads the meter every month so she's only paying for what she's using. But the temperature in her living room was 12°C over the winter because she couldn't afford to put her heating on. She used to work with old people and so had one of the thermometers that are put on pensioners walls during the winter to tell you when it's safe and when it's not. Hers was in the red – it said risk of hypothermia. So she stayed in bed and watched telly with the duvet keeping her warm.

'I used to say to the old people, "You can't afford to be cold. Put your heating on." I couldn't work out why they would think of not putting it on. But now I've come to realize just how much heating costs. You know I used to just pay the bill. It would come and I'd pay it and that was that. Now I'm thinking, I've got to turn that switch off. That plug might have residue electric in it if I don't turn the switch off. I never ever thought I'd end up thinking like that.'

On a salary of £18,000 in Manchester she lived comfortably. She went on holidays. She could go out for the day if she wanted. Now she's thinking, 'Have I got the bus fare to go into town?'

'I'm cleaning with vinegar so I don't have to buy cleaning products – that's how they used to do it and it's good enough to clean everywhere. I can't justify going in a shop and getting some Flash. The Brillo pads, I'm cutting them in half, because if you use a full one . . . you might as well use half really. If you're using half you're still getting your pan cleaned, you know what I mean? I don't throw my clothes away anymore, I use them for cleaning cloths. It makes you realize how people did live, before. But you wouldn't think in this day and age that people would have to live like that again.'

In Barnsley and Wigan, the largest employers are the council, the health service and the bus company – in that order. In some parts of the north of England, as many as one in three people work for the public sector – compared with one in six in the southeast. In October 2010 the coalition government, intent on retaining Britain's valued AAA rating with the three main credit ratings agencies, Moody's, Fitch and Standard & Poor's, began hacking away at the trembling supports that hold those jobs up. Chancellor George Osborne announced cuts of £81 billion, including £7 billion from welfare. There would be 500,000 redundancies from the government payroll with some estimating a further 500,000 hit in private companies with government or council contracts. The Institute for Fiscal Studies (IFS) has already warned that the poor will be the hardest hit. With the exception of the richest 2 per cent of the population, the IFS said, the less well off would be proportionately the hardest hit, with families with children the 'biggest losers'.

In November 2011, blaming the Eurozone crisis, George Osborne extended his austerity programme by a further two years to 2017. There were plans to borrow a further £111 billion – and continue with the cuts to corporation tax that will see it bottom out at 23 per cent in 2015. This tax cut will cost the government more than £1 billion by 2015 but, Osborne believes, will encourage the private sector to invest and provide jobs. He's publicly calculating on private companies creating enough work to lower the unemployment rate to 6 per cent. Writing for the Institute of Fiscal Studies, Mike Dicks – chief economist at Barclays Wealth, doubts this will happen. He expects unemployment to stay above 8 per cent – around the current level of 2.64 million. For the third quarter of 2011 (July to September) the budget cuts saw 135,000 people lose their jobs in the public sector – including police officers, soldiers, health workers, nurses and teachers – with 35,000 of those jobs lost in the northwest. Having benefited from the first step in Osborne's corporation tax cut in March 2011, the private sector created just 5,000 jobs nationwide. The Chartered Institute of Personnel and Development expects unemployment to rise during 2012 – and for young jobseekers to be hardest hit.

Being unemployed has rarely had such stigma attached. Whether it's in the tabloids or the pub, people living on benefits are often seen as scroungers and freeloaders. The reality is children throughout the UK going to school hungry, pensioners going without heating in winter and people trapped by circumstances beyond their control. It's poverty that takes away the choices and opportunities most of us can take for granted.

Yes, the UK benefits system is outdated and inflexible. It was designed in the 1940s. It can't cope with the temporary contracts and part-time jobs of today's workplace.

In Sheffield I met Tony, who's been living there for almost two years – having worked in Holland for a while. He's a bricklayer. In the first year he was in Holland there were loads of bricklayers from Britain, but in the second year the recession hit.

'Before the nineties you could go down to London and earn some decent money but not anymore.' He's a soft-spoken man, who leaves long pauses between sentences. Sometimes you think he's finished speaking so step in only to find he's halfway through his thought process. He notices this, and blames it on his background, brought up 'in the sticks' in a village near Huddersfield. 'There's people working for a third of the money that they should be on;. £150 a day, that's what bricklayers should be getting today. There are people without the training doing it for £50. I went on a course a couple of years ago, a forklift course. Before I went to Holland there were loads of forklift jobs, page after page at the Job Centre. They were all at least £10 an hour. I went and looked in the Job Centre today and there are no forklift jobs at all. The closest ones were Manchester but even then they'd gone down to the minimum wage. They must be handing them licences out like nothing else or there's something going on.'

Tony isn't lazy. He hates being unemployed. Everything goes downhill. He reads a lot and listens to music, tries to cut out things out like watching television through the day. He goes for long walks through the city centre and, for the last two or three months, he's even started doing voluntary work up at the cemetery, just strimming grass and stuff like that. They don't seem to give you as much stick from the Job Centre if you do stuff like that.

He went out to Holland looking for work back in 2007 and he loved it. He can name all of the twelve provinces, and even knows the names of towns down south he never went to. 'Once you've left, it's hard to come back,' he explains. 'You can feel the aggression in this country. God it were horrible coming back here and feeling that. In Holland I never heard anybody having an argument, never mind a fight.'

He would still follow the work. He'd head to Germany if he could scrape together the money for transport. He travelled to Holland on foot, which was hard getting started. Work is thin on the ground even in Germany and Tony knew not to rely on buses to get around. You need a car: 'If I had a car now I'd probably have a job,' he explains.

But there's no work. He's walked round sheffield a

dozen times just looking for work. When he first got here there was a lot of refurbishing jobs for two or three weeks. He tried it, but found it meant he had to sign off for a couple of weeks then sign on again when the job finished. It played havoc with his money – housing benefit on, then off, sign on, come off. He's renting a little one-bedroom flat now, but when he was jumping between a week here and there he couldn't keep a steady flow of money to cover the rent so he ended up in hostel accommodation.

'A hostel's no good for loads of reasons.' He takes a big gulp from his mug, finishing the contents, then stares down into his empty cup. 'I've been living a single life since I got back. It's really hard not having company of an adult there for conversation and that. And the smell of a woman, you miss that, you miss a lot of things. You can't bring someone back to a hostel. And the days of walking on to a building site and asking for a start – them jobs are few and far between. Today you need an email address. If you haven't got a car, a mobile phone, a computer, you're knackered really. You need those things just to operate. And so you need a flat. If I took agency work or temp jobs now, I'd lose the roof over my head. It's ridiculous. All I want is six months' work so I can save for a car, renew my passport then I'd be off.'

Yes, the benefit system needs reforming. It doesn't match the job market. It certainly doesn't help lift people out of poverty. The percentage of Brits in poverty has stayed roughly the same for the last ten years. The big change has been in the work/workless ratio. In the mid-1990s, the majority of those in poverty were on benefits. Today, the majority are in work. And this isn't because benefits have been soaring as scroungers live it up. The link between unemployment benefit and the UK average salary was severed in 1980, and it's been frozen for thirty years. Back then, benefit was roughly 20 per cent of average UK earnings. Today it's 10 per cent.

This brings the number of people struggling to work into sharp perspective – under the current system, a lone parent working sixteen hours at the minimum wage would only increase their take-home pay by £5 a week if they upped their hours to twenty-five. The fact that 60 per cent of single parents do have jobs is as inspiring as it is amazing. The fact that this isn't lifting them out of poverty is depressing – but it's clearly not because they're feckless and lazy.

So the government can and should change benefits for the better to ensure people get the support and opportunity they need when they need it. Right now, Tony is costing the taxpayer money – all he wants is work and a roof over his head. Sweeping welfare reforms should make that easier. Instead they're aiming to snatch even the most basic financial support from the unemployed who refuse a job, no matter what its conditions or salary. There are plans for the long-term unemployed to clean out the sewers for £1 per hour. The Welfare Bill has been making its way through parliament since February 2011, with the concept of fraudulent claimers and benefit cheats at the heart of its debate.

What's sad is that the welfare reforms began with some genuinely interesting ideas produced by Iain Duncan Smith's Centre for Social Justice – a right-of-centre think tank with an advisory board chaired by David Blunkett (whose second property in Derbyshire costs the taxpayer £600 per month, and we picked up the £1,600 cost of a new garden path) with MPs William Hague (whose mortgage interest payments of £1,200 per month picked up by the taxpayer) and Frank Field (who has received £44,338 in second home allowance between 2004 and 2008).

The proposals began with a recognition of the problems people faced getting back into work – moving from the relative security of benefits to a world of zero-hour contracts or two weeks of work then three weeks with nothing.

'It was a change in thinking,' says Moussa Haddad at Oxfam GB. 'Everyone can agree on getting people into work – people want to work, and work's not just the best route out of poverty, it's good for people's self worth. Now we're back to the old way of thinking, which is to blame people on benefits for being out of work and portray them as scroungers and fraudsters. That seems more saleable politically than the original attempt to understand the complexities of a modern economy, how that can force people into poverty and how to adjust benefits to help them into the modern workplace. The problem is, most opinion formers have jobs, proper stable jobs. For them it's a choice between a job and no job. They have no experience of the fact that things have changed, that it's just not like that for millions of people.'

At the time of writing, the Welfare Bill was still going through Parliament with one strong enlightened idea at the heart – the idea of universal benefit, where someone like Tony will have his benefit case-file left open if he gets a job, so that he's not signed off. A huge computer system should examine his PAYE slips, calculate what benefits he's entitled to and top up where needed. He won't sign off until it is clear the job is a job. In theory, he could be signing on but not getting a single penny – meaning that if something goes wrong he won't have to wait three months and lose his flat. Under Universal Credit, a lone parent shifting from sixteen hours to twenty-five hours should increase their take-home pay by £17, according to the Department for Work and Pensions (DWP).

However, the IT system hasn't been tested. In the words of a report by the Institute of Government published in March 2011, government IT systems have:

a well-documented history of too many high-profile and costly failures . . . Despite costing approximately £16bn per year, government IT seems locked in a vicious circle: struggling to get the basics right and falling further and further behind. Programmes like the National Programme for IT, the Single Payment Scheme for the Rural Payments Agency, the National Offender Management Service's C-NOMIS project and ID cards all had delivery timelines of multiple years and in some cases ended up being scrapped or radically stripped back. Slow bureaucratic processes also impede the rate of progress.

The Universal Credit system also devolves the Social Fund to local councils, who have no obligation to ring-fence any payments. The last time unemployment and housing benefits were funded regionally as opposed to nationally was in 1934 when the then coalition government disbanded the regional Public Assistance Committees because they were unfit to deal with the Depression. If we take 1936 as a benchmark, we are going backwards, not forwards.

But here's the thing – welfare frauds and benefit cheats, on the scale of the national debt reduction, will have no effect at all. In 2010 Chancellor George Osborne declared that fraud in the welfare system will not be tolerated anymore: 'We estimate that £5 billion is being lost this way each year, £5 billion that others have to work long hours to pay in their taxes. This week we published our plans to step up the fight to catch benefit cheats, and to deploy uncompromising penalties when they are.'

Which isn't strictly accurate. According to the DWP's own figures, roughly 5 per cent of benefit spend is overpaid due to 'fraud and error'. In the case of income support, for instance, of the £8.5 billion paid out in 2009–10, £460 million was fraudulently claimed or erroneously paid. Of this, under half – £210 million – was fraud. The entire benefits system – including pensions, council tax and disability – cost us £148 billion in that year; £1 billion was fraudulently claimed and £2.2 billion was overpaid in error. Focusing on sorting out mistakes would save twice as much as stopping benefit fraud. But no government of any political hue has discussed the savings to be made if we only made one error instead of two. In the same year, the DWP estimated there was a £1.3 billion under-payment – also due to fraud and error.

The fraud figure of £210 million is a lot of money. The DWP's figures show pension fraud and error coming in at £90 million – with £40 million down to official error. Pete, who lives in Speke, Liverpool, is responsible for a tiny part of that. He retired slightly early when his company closed. Although the company's pension fund survived the collapse, it took a while for the receiver to separate out the financial mess and the fund couldn't pay Pete a penny. He started claiming his state pension and his pension credits – effectively income support for retired people – and then, in 2010, his company pension started paying out. He phoned the DWP to inform them. Time passed. A bill arrived demanding he repay £2,000 in pension credits, accusing him of pension fraud. He's one of the statistics contributing to that £90 million lost through pension fraud. Is Pete's case really fraud? How much more of that £90 million is accounted for by similar cases?

Of course, to some degree, people will always nick from the government. DWP figures show that fraud accounts for less than 3 per cent of benefit payments and it's possible that some level of fiddling has always been there. 'My adolescence was spent on the Isle of Dogs in the East End, you know, before the Isle of Dogs became what it is today,' says Orwell expert Stephen Ingle. 'It really was a traditional working-class community. My mum had pneumonia when we were teenagers and she was off for four months altogether. We had a series of aunts come in and cooked and looked after us. When a friend of ours had a serious back injury, my mum, who had never done anything like it, kept his little stall for him. Now I shouldn't be saying this, but when I was a kid, and I think effectively until I was a young man, if you could pinch something from the state, you did. It was never considered pinching. From the state, that was fair game – us and them and the state was them.'

Or, as Wells Associates – accountants and business advisors in Tunbridge Wells – put it: 'In today's environment it is essential that legitimate tax planning is used to ensure that you are paying the lowest amount of tax possible.' Avoiding tax is good business sense but claiming you're single when your boyfriend actually stays over four nights a week – that's outright fraud. It's hard not to conclude that nabbing a bit from the state is different if you're rich.

Take Pauline Holt, a tired-looking fifty-two-year-old from Cross Gates in Leeds who's been unemployed for nearly two years. She worked for a sheltered housing association until she was assaulted by one of the tenants. 'He was a very big man, with very big hands, so . . . the company didn't back me – they were like, "Well, everybody has tenants like that." No, they don't. They don't have a tenant that hangs you up the wall. But they were very quick to say goodbye as well – which was a bit upsetting. I didn't have no sick cover really, which was very upsetting after being there for seven years. No backing, no sick.'

Pauline is tough; incredibly tough. She's got some elegant tattoos on her arms which she's proud to display – 'this is the only two names – apart from my grandchildren on me back, they're the two girls that sort of carried me through when I had bowel cancer' – and she worked in security at the Magistrate's Court before the housing association. She said she would work in security until she got hurt, and she did. 'But it was not an intentional hurt, not obviously,' she's quick to add. 'I got my cheekbone broke and my jawbone broke, but it wasn't something deliberate. I was in the wrong place at the wrong time. I was on a patrol with my boss at the time just as these lads from Seacroft estate with their pit bulls met a gang from Whinmoor on the corridor 'cause one of them was being sent down and the others come to gloat. There was an armed response team of fifteen police there as well and it was just a big free-for-all and I just got stuck in the middle of it. To this day I couldn't tell you who it was that did it. But I always said if I got hurt, I'd come home.'

She's happy at Cross Gate – 'it's just an average council estate really. It's got its good bits, it's got its bad bits. It's not so crime-ridden as Manchester.' But since the attack by the tenant she hasn't really gone out and about the place. She finds strangers alarming but she hasn't been to the doctor – she thinks it's just her being silly. Her plan is to sort herself out through an evening class. 'I'm going to start a painting and drawing course, as a way of getting me out of the house. The main aim is to actually get there in the first place, to the first session, because once I've met people, I know them. But,' she shrugs, 'there's worse off than me round here. Worse things and worse people in the world than me.'

She was nearly busted for benefit fraud, however, because she shared a bank account with her mother – mainly to help her mum manage her money – and because she had a boyfriend. Her mum was renting out a room in her house and paying the cash into the joint account; Pauline had split from the father of her two daughters and preferred not to take Child Support Allowance from him – which is nothing criminal, but it's unorthodox. She had a new boyfriend and someone – she mutters a name darkly – phoned the benefit fraud hotline to claim her boyfriend lived with her and she ended up in court. Until she was found not guilty, she'd been paying a little of the claimed sum back every week. Even though it is proven that she's no cheat, the council is keeping the money.

Crucially, Britain is not a work-shy country. In 1973, almost everybody had work – unemployment stood at 3 per cent. That's less than forty years ago, so almost everyone currently of working age was either already alive back then or are children of people who almost certainly had a job. Today – even in the face of short-term work, zero-hour contracts and a minimum wage that means you'd have to work for two hours to be able to stand a round of four beers in Wigan or

Manchester – Britain still isn't a work-shy country. Very few people cheat the benefit system and the residual rump that do cost the country less than tax avoidance – so how come so many people are unemployed and how come so many hard-working people are still so broke?

Because they took the jobs away. Look at Speke – dubbed Britain's Baltimore, in a reference to HBO crime drama *The Wire*, by DWP minister Chris Grayling (between 2001 and 2009, Grayling claimed for a flat in Pimlico, close to the House of Commons, despite having a constituency home less than seventeen miles away).

In 2000, Speke was the second most deprived ward in England and Wales – out of 8,414. By 2010, a report from the Joseph Rowntree Foundation warned that the Liverpool estate is 'lagging behind' other deprived areas in the north with 48 per cent of the population claiming key benefits. The foundation – an explicitly non-political research charity – seemed baffled. Speke itself, the report found, was:

> one of the most significant areas for jobs growth in Liverpool, with industrial sites to the north of the area including the Jaguar car factory, the retail offer of the New Mersey Shopping Park to the west, and the services and hospitality offer of Liverpool John Lennon Airport to the south. In theory this should offer a wealth of employment opportunities to

residents, including entry-level jobs, but work-lessness has remained stubbornly high.

Again, this wasn't always so. People used to move to Speke to get a better life. 'All they wanted was a green card for work at Fords,' says Bill, a burly man in his fifties who's lived on the estate all his life. 'You had your garden with your inside toilets, and plenty of work. You had Ford, you had Evans, you had the Metal Box, you had Lang, Dunlop, Standard Tyres, and then all the little offshoot factories, Bryant and May . . . and they all had this big supply of people.' Now there are plenty of households on the estate that spend weekends without electricity because the pre-pay key has run out.

If you look at the map of Speke you see a network of planned, criss-crossing roads and avenues enclosed by the busy A561 – Speke Boulevard – to the north, Speke Hall Avenue to the west, John Lennon Airport to the south and bleak, grey nothingness to the east. In 1933, Liverpool city architect Sir Lancelot Keay revealed plans for a radical social experiment – to create a brand new town from scratch. Keay was born in Eastbourne, Sussex, in 1883. He studied at Eastbourne College and Brighton School of Art and was appointed City Architect and Director of Housing for Liverpool in 1925. An important part of his job in the early years was overseeing the large-scale clearance of slum housing in the city.

In the 1920s, before Keay descended, Speke was a collection of rolling fields and small farmhouses. Sir Lancelot described his idea ffor the area as a 'magic carpet'. The new town would accommodate around 20,000 people with all necessary facilities as if it had grown naturally over the years. 'I feel that what we need is something different from the old method of building cottages without any playgrounds and without any spaces for recreation,' he said at the time.

His proposals included 5,000 houses, a technical school, a parish church, public baths and a community centre with concert hall, gymnasium, public library, cinemas, art gallery and open-air theatre.

The estate was planned as a self-contained community unit. A new industrial estate alongside the housing estate would provide work for the new residents. By the late 1950s, Speke's population had boomed to more than 25,000 and it was a model for self-contained municipal housing estates throughout the world.

You can measure Speke's decline in pop songs. 'In My Liverpool Home' – a song made famous by the Spinners and written in 1962 – includes the following verse: 'When I grew up, I met Bridget McCann; she said, "You're not much, but I'm needing a man; I want sixteen kids, and a house out in Speke"; well, the flesh it was willing, but the spirit was weak . . .'

A few years later, the song's writer – folk musician

Peter McGovern – had changed his view of the place. 'Rent Collecting in Speke' charts the hapless Willie Moran, 'of yellow he'd never a streak; Hunted shark, fished for whale, and he never turned tail, till he tried rent-collecting in Speke'. Willie tries a flamethrower, a tank and armed guards but winds up in hospital with the staff nurse grinning – 'he's been rent-collecting in Speke . . .'

If you wanted to spin it that way, you could describe Speke in the same way today. On a sunny afternoon mooch, Bill and I walked towards the airport along wide, tree-lined and largely empty boulevards. Every so often men would come striding along the otherwise deserted pavements, always wiry, intent and – it being the one hot day of the summer – shirtless. Most of them had tattoos of some kind – small, blue tattoos in the old tradition, no sprawling Celtic flounces or colourful sleeves of ink.

We watched a mother telling off a boy who looked to be maybe twelve years old, wearing a football shirt and scruffy trainers. The kid had a piece of wood – it looked as if it was a long shard splintered from a forklift palate or fence. One end had a jagged point. 'Give it to me,' the mother yelled, pursuing the boy off the pavement and on to the wide tarmac of the road, her voice strained with anger. The boy hesitated and it seemed as if he might make a dash for it. Then he reconsidered, handed it to her and mumbled something as we walked past. She began to tell him off, clearly settling in to a long tirade and dragging him away.

We walked down Eastern Avenue and stopped outside the Orient Hotel – a large, red brick pub with steel shutters drawn more than halfway down, as if expecting a riot. They used to bring the shutters down at 6 p.m. – not because the pub was shut, but because there could be trouble – but these days they don't bother raising them. There are few pubs in the UK that talk proudly of events like the Fruit Machine Riot of 1983.

Just beyond the Orient a high wooden fence blocks the end of Eastern Avenue. In the 1970s this used to be the entrance to the Ford factory. Thousands of men would spill out through those gates at lunchtime, in the evening, at the end of every shift. Regulars would have their food and pint waiting for them at the Orient. There used to be a butcher's, a chemist and a newsagent opposite. Now as we stand outside the parade of shops, Bill looks uncomfortable. 'Put your notebook away,' he says quietly, evenly, not looking at me. 'You look like a DWP spotter.'

'When I left school in 1978 everything just went,' he remembers as we stare at the pale wood that now blocks the old factory gates. 'My generation had kids, some of them have got kids now and some people have never worked. We lost all the jobs – it just went, it was wiped out. In the space of three years we'd lost nearly everything. Dunlop had gone. Standards had gone. Ford had cut jobs, the Metal Box was on its way to closing down. They just disappeared. Absolutely disappeared. Apprenticeships went, so then we had the training schemes, and that's all we had. That's how we survived it here on in – everything gone in the space of five years. During that period all they wanted to do was chop us off and let us float away into the Mersey.'

When they redeveloped John Lennon airport they built a Holiday Inn Express just down the road, a new Premier Inn and a Marriott. But recruitment isn't local – it's citywide. Just like the Jaguar plant, which expanded on Speke Boulevard and employed, in total, one person from Speke's 16,000 residents. In part this is purely technical. The Jaguar job application – like most applications – required an online form. Laptops aren't big in Speke, broadband uptake is low and there aren't any internet cafés.

All the same, Marion got work at the airport. Marion is twenty-two, has five GCSE's and an NVQ in customer care. She applied for a job at the Marriott Hotel and was offered a zero-hour contract in a deal that reeks of the dockers' pen Orwell found in Liverpool, where casual dockers were herded into a cage each morning to beg for a day's work. Zero-hour contracts guarantee the employee nothing – zero hours per week – so Marion had to turn up at the hotel every day to see if they had anything for her to do. If not, she'd be sent home without pay. In 2010, seventeen workers at Paragon Automotive in Stallingborough, South Humberside, sued their employer for unfair dismissal and won an out-of-court settlement after Paragon forced them on to zero-hour contracts in place of their former forty to forty-five-hour-per-week contracts.

Marion took the job. It meant she was no longer eligible for income support but she took the contract anyway – even though it took her off benefits without actually agreeing definitely to pay her anything. She took it because she wanted to work. For the first three days, they sent her home because her immediate superior was too busy to train her. Her first shift was 5 p.m. on Christmas Eve to midnight on Christmas Day.

'In the end, there was just no money,' she explains. 'I was off benefits and getting no pay. How long can you hold on? The debts were building up. I had to jack the job and sign on. Which meant I was sanctioned for leaving a job – six weeks on a crisis loan. I was starving. One day I was too tired to lift the bin because I hadn't had anything solid to eat for two days. You go into the shop and you can see the loan sharks hovering, working out if you're going to ask for something on tick. Then they tap you up outside.'

Another woman went for a job as a female security guard in the airport, checking women who beeped on the metal detector as they went through. She thought –

probably loads of overtime, even though it was a zero-hour contract. She worked 364 days then they laid her off for two days, just so she didn't have a year in employment. No sick pay, no annual leave. Her friend got a job with a housing provider on the other side of Liverpool. At the interview they encouraged her to buy an annual bus travelcard, so she borrowed money to buy one – then, before she started, they told her they'd overestimated the people they needed and she needn't turn up. They told her by text.

The number of households in which no adult has ever worked rose 5 per cent between 2010 and 2011 to 297,000 – the highest in a decade, according to official figures. The biggest previous figure, 284,000, was recorded between April and June 2008. Northeast England had the highest percentage of workless households, with one-quarter of homes in the area falling into this category. The southeast had the lowest numbers, with one in seven households classed as workless. If people talk about reckless hoodies and the need for national service, maybe they're missing the obvious point.

'If you got a job at Ford, an apprenticeship after leaving school, you'd work alongside older people, people who knew your mum and dad,' Bill points out. 'If you got out of line, they tell your ma and you'd get a slap. It taught discipline. It taught people to grow up. People used to grow up next to factories and pits.

Now they grow up next to superstores and shopping malls.'

The government's solution for workless households – according to employment minister Chris Grayling (who also owned two buy-to-let properties in Wimbledon whilst we paid for his London flat – with his 2005 refit and redecoration the total cost to the taxpayer came to £104,183) – is the Work Programme, essentially the provision of back-to-work and training schemes parcelled out to private companies who will be paid by results, meaning getting people off benefits.

Ingeus Deloitte, A4e, Seetec, Avanta, G4S and Working Links divvy up the lion's share of the regional Work Programmes between them. G4S is a private security company that runs prisons in the UK as well as security and protection contracts in Algeria, Rwanda, Afghanistan and Sudan and private policing deals in Cape Town, South Africa. Perhaps as a result, it has a fairly blunt way of dealing with the facts for the Work Programme. Sean Williams, managing director of G4S's welfare-to-work programme, conceded that the job market had changed since the contracts were outlined. 'Is the [bonus] target realistic? My answer would be no,' he told the *Financial Times*. 'Any organisation which built their contract around hitting that bonus might well be unsuccessful.'

All the same, these companies are going to give those targets a damn good try. Seetec, for instance, was running back-to-work programmes for Job Centres under the previous government. Norman Charles, a twenty-eight-year-old would-be-entrepreneur from Birmingham, was recently placed on a programme run by Seetec.

'When I first heard the news, I thought great . . . maybe finally I'll actually get some help,' he explains. 'I've got great PC skills and I'm good at running servers and setting up websites. All I actually lack is a piece of paper to say that I can do it. I've been trying to work out the details of setting up a new business over the past few months.

'At Seetec, I was met by a Mark Smith, from the Seetec office in Birmingham city centre. I explained all this to him – that I am keen on setting up a business and need some help finalizing the plans – particularly in regards to VAT and all the rest of it. He checked my Jobseekers agreement and said that they can only help me find work that I've stated I'm looking for on that – and that the only help they could give me in regards to setting up my own business is £300 that they have sitting around the office. For one thing, I didn't ask for any money . . . and for another, £300 is quite a laughable amount to offer somebody setting up a business . . . unless I went into drug dealing. So why offer me £300? Obviously because if I took it I'd be signed off due to his good work then he would be in line for some bonuses and doubtless his company would be in line for even bigger bonuses.

'Then he went on to tell me that I will have to do four weeks' work in a factory, for free . . . that's going to keep me on benefits when all I want to do is set up my own business. I declined to sign his Action Plan committing me to work experience in a factory and I was then, of course, instantly sanctioned. I appealed on the sanction more than four weeks ago and still haven't heard a thing back. Meanwhile, I get another letter from Seetec asking me to come in again so we can go over what I've done to fulfil my part in the Action Plan I never signed. I am still waiting on the outcome of my appeal so don't see why I should attend, particularly when the reason for attendance is going over what I've done to fulfil the requirements of an Action Plan I never signed. It's madness.

'I then do some more legwork and find a real company offering help, but I need to be recommended by a Job Centre advisor. I telephone Selly Oak Job Centre and they tell me that they can't refer me as I am with Seetec and they will have to do it. I have to do what I'm told. All I want to do is get a little help setting up my business, just some professional advice is all I need and I will sign off within the month. But it's impossible. It's crazy.'

When a Job Centre staffer blew his whistle to the *Guardian* in April 2011, he explained how these little tricks worked. 'If you want someone to diversify – they're an electrician or a plumber, they may not want to go into call centres or something,' he explained. 'What you do is keep promoting such and such a job, and you pressure them into taking it off you, the piece of paper. Then in two weeks you look at the system, you ask them if they applied for it . . . they say no – you stop their money for six months.'

There are easier ways of bringing the unemployment numbers down. Although the story has run its course for most news outlets, the spontaneous outrage at the government's wilful shedding of jobs at Bombardier – the last train-building factory in the UK – is still seething.

In June 2011 the Department of Transport awarded a £1.5 billion contract to build new Thameslink trains to a consortium led by Siemens, which meant the carriages would be built in Germany. As a consequence, Derby-based Bombardier announced 1,400 redundancies with its long-term UK future in doubt. Across the country, from cab drivers in Wigan to pensioners in Bradford, people cite Bombardier as an example of all that's wrong in the UK – a callous government ignoring the people and their need for work. But it's actually much worse.

The details of the contract are not in the public domain – because it has suited successive governments to keep these things hidden. What we do know is that it wasn't an old-school 'we'll buy those trains off you' contract. It was a private finance initiative (PFI)-style contract, which covered the building of the carriages plus their maintenance, plus the lease finance, for thirty years. A summary of the tender in April 2008 states: 'the chosen bidder will be required to arrange the finance necessary for the acquisition and ownership of the rolling stock'.

Interestingly, it is the credit agencies Standard & Poor's, Fitch and Moody's who shoulder some of the blame here. This was never going to be a level playing field when Siemens had an A+ credit rating and Bombardier a BB+. On a back-of-an-envelope calculation (and in the absence of information from the government) this probably gave Siemens a finance cost advantage of around £500 million to £700 million.

In other words, an important decision about jobs and the UK engineering skill was all mixed up financially with the happenstance of the credit rating of the foreign company. Credit ratings are biased towards established, giant firms and against newcomers. Successful, conservative, giant companies like Siemens will always have better credit ratings than struggling, publicly listed companies like Bombardier, new entrants and start-ups. David Cameron and George Osborne talk about the small British companies of today becoming the giants of tomorrow whilst drawing up contracts that actively prevent that happening.

In September 2011, transport secretary Phil Hammond refused yet again to review the decision, saying the Siemens deal was the best value for the taxpayer. But Karel Williams and his team at the Center for Economic Research and Social Change (CERSC), an economic think tank in Manchester, argue that, if you take into account the lost tax revenue from choosing a non-British factory and the British private sector's inability to create extra jobs and employment in companies supplying Bombardier, the Siemens decision represents terrible value for the taxpayer.

First, the tax receipts from the workers at the Derby factory now become the German government's tax receipts. From company accounts, Bombardier Transportation's average labour cost was nearly £60,000 per worker in 2009 – so that the total employee and employer tax payment per employee is a massive £16,989. And this excludes more than £10,000 per year to the Bombardier pension scheme – which is, of course, a long-term investment in reducing the dependence of the elderly on state support. Williams assumes that the Thameslink contract would involve 1,000 jobs, giving us nearly £20 million per year by 2012 and increasing each year with inflation and real wages.

Most free-market economists reject this thinking – arguing jobs and industries come and go as the market decides and you can't buck the market. The decline of the horse-buggy industry was an issue for its employees but the rise of the car industry more than compensated.

The closure of a rail factory in Derby doesn't matter because wind turbines – or whatever – will replace the lost jobs. Creative destruction.

But over the boom of the last decade, the vast majority of new jobs were created by the government and the private sector isn't replacing them. In the northwest, 38 per cent of new jobs were in the private sector. In the West Midlands, private-sector jobs fell by 79 per cent. The only region with strong private-sector, full-time job growth is London and there is little movement to London from the rest of the UK. In Germany manufacturing output is currently increasing at 14 per cent per annum. 'Given the historical record of the British private sector since the first Thatcher recession and its current dark prospects, the working principle in the UK right now should be to maintain whatever jobs it can,' says Williams.

Williams goes further – even if Bombardier kept the contract, many of the parts assembled in Derby would have been made in Germany, thanks to the constant refusal by governments of both political hue to invest in the national rail network. In the mid-1980s, British Rail Engineering Limited (BREL) produced the InterCity 125, the InterCity 225 and various smaller models. The 125 was the world's fastest diesel train when built and is still in service today. It wasn't world class but it was a good place to start and was an entirely viable industry. Governments refused to build high-speed rail links, refused to electrify any main lines except the East Coast and resolutely avoided spending any money modernizing a collapsing commuter network.

In 1989 BREL was privatized and got snapped up by Swiss-Swedish conglomerate ABB. In 1999 ABB sold to DaimlerChrysler Rail Systems. Two years later Daimler sold its European operations to Canada's Bombardier. By 2001 Derby's record was five changes of ownership and at least three changes of management systems and objectives in twelve years. At the same time, British rolling-stock orders were interrupted by rail privatization and then became erratically variable ever afterwards. Bankers and civil servants had created a Balkanized system of train operating companies: with leased rolling stock so that paying someone money to build a train became almost impossible.

The result was an impossibly erratic flow of orders to the shop floor and 'pass the parcel' rapid changes of private ownership by foreign conglomerates whose British operations were side shows. British plants were never integrated into European corporate parents and survived as branch assemblers until they were closed when the flow of British orders dried up. One rail engineering factory after another shut down. First York, then – in 2005 – GEC Alstom ran out the last of fifty-three Pendolino electric trains and closed its 150-year-old plant in Birmingham. That left Bombardier Derby.

'British politicians and civil servants insisted that ownership does not matter when changes in ownership and order-book fluctuations were wrecking the train-building industry,' Williams argues.

Here's the question. In the UK who is it that actually believes that the decision to award the contract to Siemens was a good idea? Even the coalition ministers responsible distance themselves from the decision. We've shown that it doesn't make sense economically. But this leads us to the real puzzle. Why don't the politicians and their unhappy civil servants also see this? Why are they unable to make calculations of the kind that we've made? How have they got themselves in the position where 'best buy' 'value for money' calculations lead them inexorably to such an economically catastrophic industrial train crash? The empirics are there already in the company reports and official statistics. There is a straightforward incapacity on the part of Britain's politicians and civil servants to practise matter-of-fact political arithmetic. How come those who govern us can't, or won't, do this? And why must the train workers of Derby pick up their P45s in 2011, just like those from Birmingham in 2005?

The business model that caused these problems – heavy borrowing and aggressive acquisitions by companies with no assets but fixed liabilities – is troubling when it comes to jobs, but it's terrifying when it comes to life and death issues such as health. The catastrophe of Southern Cross nursing homes raised this threat – but that is only the tip of a malignant iceberg threatening all our health.

CHAPTER 6

Food

When I was a small boy at school a lecturer used to come once a term and deliver excellent lectures on famous battles of the past, such as Blenheim, Austerlitz, etc. He was fond of quoting Napoleon's maxim 'An army marches on its stomach', and at the end of his lecture he would suddenly turn to us and demand, 'What's the most important thing in the world?' We were expected to shout 'Food!' and if we did not do so he was disappointed.

George Orwell, *The Road to Wigan Pier*, 1936

'It's horrible, trying to live on £50 a week,' Brian mumbles into his hands as he presses his fingers gently against his temples. 'I've got a really crap diet at the moment. I like to eat loads of vegetables and fruit and that. There's times I haven't anything like that in. You can't buy anything fresh really, you need money every day to buy fresh. It's all tinned things now. At times it's just beans on toast.'

The Trussell Trust is a Christian charity that operates food banks – the modern equivalent of Salvation Army soup kitchens. Using churches as the hubs of its operation, the Trust hands out food parcels containing roughly three days' worth of food. It's all tinned or dry – the charity calls it 'a nutritionally balanced, non-perishable ration' – and it all comes in through donations, largely from churchgoers. To claim your parcel you need a voucher given out by a doctor, social worker, council housing officer or other frontline care professionals deemed qualified to identify people in crisis. This helps filter out the blaggers looking for a free lunch.

In Bradford, Trussell operates out of the Lighthouse Church – a new evangelical church based at a converted school on Jermyn Street. Gareth, a wiry, earnest young Welshman with a dry sense of humour and a strong sense of faith, showed me around at high speed – 'it's my Challenge Aneka moment,' he cried, as I puffed behind him. He stopped briefly to show me the interview room, the crèche, the clothes store, the kitchen and a large room filled with shelves all stacked with tins of soup, tuna and peaches. It looked like a densely packed corner store. Another young man raced past and Gareth waved at him with one hand – 'he's a burglar. Fortunately he's only taking the rubbish. You can tell he's from Bradford . . .'

We picked through some pre-wrapped bags on the floor, laid out according to a single person's need or a family's need. A single person's parcel, for instance, consists of:

One small packet of cereal
Two cans of soup
Two small tins of baked beans
Two small tins of tomatoes
Two small tins of vegetables
Two small tins of meat or vegetarian alternative
One small tin of fish
Two small tins of fruit
One tin of rice pudding
One small packet of biscuits
500 g sugar
500 g pasta
40 tea bags
One carton of juice
One carton of UHT milk

For a family, the food parcel, which comes in a shopping bag, weighs about 40 kg – meaning twelve parcels come to roughly half a tonne of food. People come through Gareth's doors for all sorts of reasons – redundancy, illness, benefit delay or sanction, domestic violence, debt, family breakdown and winter heating bills. Most aren't homeless – although he has helped out an Afghanistan veteran living on the streets. They are usually low-income working families facing a redundancy or benefits crisis. Recently, for instance, he helped a family where dad was on a zero-hour contract, fell ill and had no money coming in; he also helped a woman on the run from a situation so grave he begged me not to list any details, in case someone spotted her story and knew he'd stepped in.

By July 2011, Gareth had been running the Trussell Trust's food bank for six months and reckoned around twelve new people walked through the door every week – he'd served more than 300 people, in other words, and he'd been keeping that number low by limiting the number of vouchers given out. 'We'd be swamped otherwise,' he explained, bounding up another flight of stairs.

At national level, the Trussell Trust is stretched equally thin. In the first half of 2011 it was opening new food banks at the rate of one per week and served 61,500 people, a number that had been rising steadily – 26,000 in 2008–9, 41,000 in 2009–10. Chairman Chris Mould predicts they could be serving 500,000 by 2015 if things continue as they are.

'Food bank clients are faced with impossible choices between paying the rent and buying food,' he explained. 'Parents skip meals or consider crime to feed their children. The shocking truth is that thousands are going hungry in their own homes in twenty-first-century Britain.'

In 1936, malnutrition was still a problem in England. In 1937, poverty researcher Boyd Orr identified the survival point below which malnutrition set in to be eight shillings – or about 40p per person per week. The need for healthy soldiers, free milk in schools from 1934 and the quality control of rationing meant that by the end of the Second World War – according to a government report – 'the average diet of all classes was better balanced than ever before'. Since then, thanks to cheaper food, refrigerators and reasonable income, malnutrition simply hasn't been an issue. In March 2011, however, the charity Bapen found that one in three people admitted to hospital were suffering from malnutrition – usually the elderly.

Those poor souls were suffering from malnutrition as we all understand it – they were literally starving to death. In the past few years, however, the term 'Modern Malnutrition' has entered the medical lexicon to describe diets with dangerously high levels of fat, sugar and salt. Poor diet contributes to almost 50 per cent of deaths from heart disease, one-third of all cancer deaths, low birthweight, and childhood morbidity and mortality. There is also growing evidence to support the link between poor diets and antisocial behaviour. In a placebo-controlled study in men's prison, vitamin, mineral and essential fatty acid supplements reduced incidents of serious violence by almost 40 per cent.

In a report for the Royal College of Physicians, Lindsey Stewart of the Faculty of Public Health warned that:

> people on low incomes eat more processed foods which are much higher in saturated fats and salt. They also eat less variety of foods. This is related to economies of scale and fear of potential waste. People living on state benefits eat less fruit and vegetables, less fish and less high-fibre breakfast cereals. People in the UK living in households without an earner consume more total calories, and considerably more fat, salt and non-milk extrinsic sugars than those living in households with one or more earners.

Of course, it's easy to argue that obesity is not our problem – it's the fault of the person who isn't eating well. Who cares if they're poor or not? But Orwell knew the score back in 1936. He found that the miners' diet was 'appalling':

> the basis of their diet is white bread and margarine, corned beef, sugared tea, and potatoes. Would it not be better if they spent more money on wholesome things like oranges and wholemeal

bread or if they even, like the writer of the letter to the New Statesman, saved on fuel and ate their carrots raw?

Yes, it would, but the point is that no ordinary human being is ever going to do such a thing. The ordinary human being would sooner starve than live on brown bread and raw carrots. And the peculiar evil is this, that the less money you have, the less inclined you feel to spend it on whole-some food. A millionaire may enjoy breakfasting off orange juice and Ryvita biscuits; an unem-ployed man doesn't. When you are unemployed, underfed, harassed, bored, and miserable, you don't want to eat dull wholesome food. You want something a little bit 'tasty'.

The rush of carbohydrates from a white bread, potatoes and corned beef diet makes sense if you're buying cheap calories for a day of hard physical work in a mine. The same diet for that miner's unemployed children is, however, a fast track to obesity. But with low incomes eaten away by fuel and food price inflation it's the cost of food that takes precedence over issues of taste and healthy eating.

The Joseph Rowntree Foundation's Minimum Income Standard suggests a food budget of £46 per week for a single person or £112 for a couple with children – based on the idea that a single person needs (ignoring rent and council tax) £170 a week as a minimum and the couple need £403. Lisa, who lives at the edge of Liverpool's Croxteth Park estate, gets £134 per week. After paying all her essentials – gas, water, electricity, TV licence, bus fares, new socks – the week we go shopping she's got, effectively, £6.50 per day to spend on food for her and her five-year-old daughter, Kaya. We head to Iceland, sprawling in a retail park just off East Lancashire Road. Ten cod fishcakes, frozen chips and a kilo of frozen peas come to £3, a box of chicken wings cost another £3 and she's got one day covered.

'Kaya likes a lot a lot of attention,' she explains as we pause in the aisle. 'She's gobby. Typical five-year-old. If I don't give her the food she likes, she doesn't eat it. It's a waste. I can't afford to chuck stuff away. I grew up to a single mum, also on benefits. She was restricted to what stuff she could buy – we had chips and beans, chips and egg, chips and sausage, chips and something every day. If we were lucky on Sunday we'd get a tiny bit of meat. We used to get a takeaway or a kebab because it's easier. I started off like that – I'd had my cooker a full year before I turned it on, I didn't even know it had two ovens. And now I try to cook and get her to cook with me.'

She does everything she can to preserve Kaya's food money. If there's a shock – something breaks or she has to buy a present – she'll cut down herself rather than have Kaya eat less. There's a woman two doors down who had a bit of trouble with borrowing and is trying to pay someone back – she doesn't invite her own daughter over at the moment because she can't afford to give her a cup of tea. Just for now, until the debts are paid. One day she asked Lisa to help her put the bin bags out because she felt really weak and pathetic. It turned out she'd only had a packet of digestive biscuits to eat over the past three days.

There are numbers proving exactly how much money we could save as a country if we helped people eat well. In February 2010 Professor Sir Michael Marmot, of University College London, published the Marmot Review – the findings of a team of medical experts looking at health inequality in the UK. Many of his conclusions were startling but one stands out: if everyone in England had the same death rates as the most advantaged, people who are currently dying young thanks to health inequalities would, in total, have enjoyed between 1.3 and 2.5 million extra years of life. They would, in addition, have had a further 2.8 million years free of limiting illness or disability.

'In England, people living in the poorest neighbourhoods, will, on average, die seven years earlier than people living in the richest neighbourhoods while the average difference in disability free life expectancy is 17 years,' he wrote. 'People in poorer areas not only die sooner, but they also spend more of their shorter lives with a disability. Even excluding the poorest five per cent and the richest five per cent the gap in life expectancy between low and high income is six years, and in disability-free life expectancy 13 years.'

It's not just about being fair. Taking one small part of Marmot's review – the cost of treating the various illnesses that result from inequalities in the level of obesity alone – we find costs of £2 billion per year rising to nearly £5 billion per year in 2025.

Marmot estimated that inequality in illness accounts for productivity losses of £31 billion to £33 billion per year, as well as lost taxes and higher welfare payments in the range of £20 billion to £32 billion per year, and NHS healthcare costs in excess of £5.5 billion per year. At the high end of his estimates, that is roughly £70 billion per year or £350 billion over five years. George Osborne's £80 billion cuts will take five years in total – averaging out at £16 billion per year. Ending health inequality would cover the cost of those cuts and give us £55 billion in change.

GP Dr Douglas Hold was born in Manchester – himself the son of a GP, so it almost runs in the blood. He's nearing retirement and is about as decent a doctor as it's possible to find. The practice – founded back in the 1930s – still does the occasional house call, although far fewer than he'd like. He's got the perfect bedside manner, though, listening intently – as I describe a mishap on the way to his surgery – with the carefully nodding smile of a man used to letting patients talk about stressful situations. He's conservatively dressed with hair cropped short and looks exactly how Pete Postlethwaite would have looked if he were playing a village doctor. Although it's clear he's an almost instinctive doctor, he still seems to take each of my questions carefully, considering each sentence and often pausing for some time as he gathers his thoughts. At one point I ask what he feels proudest of in his thirty years in practice and he takes so long to reply that I almost ask the question again.

'I don't know exactly what effect I've had,' he ventures finally. 'I couldn't say for sure if I've directly made any difference. I might have a patient who gives up smoking and I've prescribed nicotine replacement but I couldn't say if that's really what helped. People come to me and I have ten minutes of their life and the only thing I really know for sure is that the first thing I think as they walk through the door is probably wrong.'

His practice is large and busy – ten GPs in a large health centre near the former industrial heartland of the city – and he's been a partner since the early 1980s. East Manchester was once the metal-bashing district of the city, with steelworks and engineering firms swallowing up acres of land. After the factories closed, the East Manchester Initiative spent most of the 1980s and £9 million on acquiring and demolishing derelict industrial buildings. Next came the East Manchester Partnership, which bid for the Olympics in 1992 and 2000 but settled for the Commonwealth Games in 2002. Since then, there's been the Pathfinder Programme and some supermarkets and that's about it.

'There have always been the problems of smoking, there have always been the problems of drinking and there have always been the problems of people feeling isolated, feeling that they have nothing to do and feeling worthless,' he explains carefully. 'Those sorts of people and those sorts of problems are still around and always have been. Some of the people who sadden me the most are the young people that get into alcohol in such a big way that they can't get out of it – it's more of a destructive drug than heroin in the number of people it kills and the effect is has on their lives.'

By way of illustration, he says, 'One guy I treated had a chronic anxiety problem and was always coming in about various symptoms that he had and couldn't work because of his anxiety. He was a very decent, sensible guy but had these anxiety problems and he drank as well. At first, I didn't know about it but then he was seeing the community alcohol team. But he couldn't stop and it killed him. His family were devastated, his partner was devastated – she couldn't believe that I and other services couldn't help him. There was a woman with some family problems who was working at Tesco but was unable to hold down the job because of the alcohol – a very decent woman but she couldn't stop drinking and it killed her. There was a woman with a young child who denied her drinking all the way up to the point where she had cirrhosis and a bloated abdomen, jaundice. She was still denying it as it killed her. So it's great sadness when alcohol gets a hold.'

As mentioned earlier, it's not the poor who drink. In the most recent data from the Office for National Statistics, it's managerial and professional households where both men and women drink heavily – the higher your income, the more you drink. In homes with an average weekly income of £1,000 or above, men throw back nineteen units and women eleven units a week whilst in houses with an income of lower than £200 per week, men drink sixteen units and women drink six units a week. Students drink far more than the unemployed. In fact, in unemployed households, booze consumption drops right off. The chances of someone with a job having a drink in a typical week are roughly 70 per cent. For the unemployed, it's 50 per cent. An accurate documentary about booze-binge Britain would focus on the middle classes drinking at home.

All the same, the most recent figures – from 2009 – show alcohol-related deaths are much higher among unskilled men than professionals. At the same time, alcohol-related deaths are far higher in the northwest of England than the rest of the country – 23 per 100,000 deaths for men and 12 per 100,000 for women against a national average of 17 deaths per 100,000 people for men and 8 for women.

This means that, even though it's the middle classes who drink heavily and who drink more dangerous kinds of booze – wine and spirits versus lager – it's working-class men in deprived regions who are most likely to be killed by alcohol, in part through generally poorer health but also because drinking tends to be in binges, brief bursts of heavy drinking as opposed to constant levels of medium to heavy drinking in middle-class men, which puts greater strain on the heart.

The poorer you are, the greater the damage caused by drink and by each individual cigarette. Research from the 2002 health survey for England found social deprivation effectively caused higher levels of nicotine intake – an average of 30 per cent higher in the most deprived smokers versus the most affluent smokers. This is partly due to poorer smokers smoking more, but also down to the intensity with which each cigarette is smoked. The northwest is the smoking capital of England – 23 per cent of adults smoke compared to 18 per cent in the southwest.

In fact, living in the northwest of England is not good for your health at all. In 2010, the northwest had the highest death rate in England – 11 per cent above the national average, whilst London and the southeast came in at 7 per cent below the national average. Liverpool was the easiest place to die – 35 per cent above the national average – whilst Kensington and Chelsea is the healthiest place to live at 41 per cent below the national average. If you live on the Hunts Cross side of Speke Boulevard your average life expectancy is ten years higher than for someone living in Speke. This, as the Office for National Statistics points out, is largely due to 'income deprivation, socio-economic status and health behaviour'.

It may not be surprising then to find that in the northwest of England, young men are killing themselves at a staggering rate. Over the past ten years, the most common suicide victims have been young men under the age of twenty-four and the number of suicides has risen sharply since the recession began. Suicide rates overall, but especially rates for young men, are highest in the northwest and northeast of England – with twenty young men killing themselves for every 100,000 people in the area and nineteen per 100,000 people respectively. The regions with the lowest rates were London and the east of England.

The health service is as puzzled as it is alarmed by these deaths. The majority of these men have not asked for help before they took their own life, so any guess at why can only be a guess. Doctors do know that the suicide rate tends to rise and fall with the unemployment rate in a number of countries – half of the record 33,000 people who committed suicide in Japan in 1999 were unemployed. Then there's social isolation: those who kill themselves often live alone and have little contact with others.

And this recession has been tough on the young. The unemployment rate for sixteen to twenty-four year-olds has risen sharply, from 15 per cent in 2008 to 19 per cent in 2009 and then to 20 per cent in 2010. As a result, the unemployment rate for sixteen to twenty-four year-olds in 2010 was actually higher than its previous peak in 1993. The unemployment rate for this age group is now more than three times the rate for older workers – by contrast, in the mid-1990s, it was twice that rate. Two-fifths of all those who are unemployed are now aged under twenty-five and the figure is higher for young men than young women.

Before starting work on this book, I spent a week in a mortuary in Edinburgh. The first body I saw sliced open on the slab was a suicide. The victim was young, maybe twenty-four years old. He had a girl's name tattooed on his arm – someone he'd loved. His head was flung back and his arms stretched out and when they tried to move him, it was like moving a rubber doll. His limbs stayed fixed in place, making it hard to fit him on the narrow, silver table. Around his throat was a thin blue cord tied so tightly that the skin had folded over it. Frayed ends led off to the point where the policeman had cut him down, releasing his body from the tree from which he'd chosen to hang himself.

The pathologist flicked through a slim brown folder of notes. The boy was a drinker, a depressive, a bit of a troublesome loner. His school career was messy and he'd drifted a lot afterwards. He'd tried to get himself back on the straight and narrow a few times and finally he was getting treatment. Briefly, it was looking like he'd turned the corner but then, over the weekend, he'd been found dead in the grounds of a Salvation Army hospital.

The three shining metal tables in the white, operating theatre-style room had been working constantly through the morning – perhaps twelve bodies so far. When I'd arrived outside the modern, square building in the heart of Edinburgh's gothic old town I had never seen a single corpse. After one day I felt like a veteran. I'd been astonished at how quickly the process of a post-mortem is normalized.

The description sounds brutal. First, the pathologist makes a cut across the back of the head and peels forward the skin until the face is almost off. Using an electric saw they cut open the skull and remove and weigh the brain, then return it and seal everything back up again.

After that, they move to the torso, cutting it open and working through all the internal organs, weighing, slicing and measuring. They take samples and look at them under a microscope. They probe into the liver and the pancreas for signs and clues as to how the person on the slab met their end. After they've processed all possible medical indicators, they replace everything almost tenderly and sew the wound up with the care a surgeon might give to a living patient. I'd expected gallows humour, but mostly they worked with quiet precision – two or three white-coated pathologists to a table, reading numbers from electronic scales to each other; 'Heart 260 grams.'

Perhaps it's this routine that gradually quashes your first, instinctive horror and nausea – although, for some reason, you never stop finding fat repulsive. As it spills out of a distended belly like cold, yellow custard, it seems so clearly wrong, so obviously the product of a stop-gap biological process that your guts rebel every time. Fortunately, modern post-mortem suites are designed to conceal the smell – something that used to be impossible to ignore. The three bulky steel tables give off a low hum as machines in the basement suck down the air above them, dragging down the odour of decomposition.

The stench was ever present, though, because bodies arrive here some time after death. Most of us don't end on the slab. Most death certificates are signed by GPs, or by hospital doctors who attend the final hours of the recently deceased. In such cases the cause of death is well known and the signature is easy to come by. For a thousand years, however, the state has wanted to know how every one of its citizens died. Every corpse needs a signature. Every death needs a reason.

The morgue is a Victorian update of a system established by Alfred the Great. It's the place where certain deaths are resolved – those where the cause is unclear or is the result of some intended or accidental violence. The bodies are almost always victims in some way – of crime, suicides and car crashes, but also victims of loneliness. It's where you go if you die alone in your flat and your body lies undisturbed for days. It's where you go if no one knew you were dying and no GP attended your final hours. It's where you go if no loved one held your hand as you slipped away. In one way or another, then, all the people who pass through this room are the people who die screaming.

This morgue's master is Professor Anthony Busuttil, a confident, jolly man in his late sixties, with dark hair and twinkling eyes. He is Regius Professor of Forensic Medicine at the University of Edinburgh and a clinical forensic medical examiner for the Lothian and Borders police. He was also the pathologist on the ground at the Lockerbie disaster. He's worked here for nineteen years dealing with a fairly constant workload – some forty bodies a week or just over 2,000 a year in a city of half a million souls. In the last five years, however, he's noticed a change in the pattern of his work.

'The deaths have become tinged with such despair,'

he says. 'There are more suicides than there used to be. Suicide used to be the prerogative of the young – eighteen to twenty-five year olds. Now we're seeing suicides right up to the seventies. We're also seeing more and more bodies that have been lying around for weeks. More than ever before, people are dying at home, on their own, and nobody cares. No neighbours have knocked. No one has taken a blind bit of notice. We are, without doubt, becoming less and less of a caring society.'

Over Christmas, these deaths are at their peak. Suicides, home-alone corpses, drug- and alcohol-related deaths and murders all spike during the season of goodwill. In the post-Christmas week I spent with him, for instance, Busuttil saw an eighteen-year-old who died of a drugs overdose, a fifty-two-year-old autistic man who died of bronchial pneumonia, a forty-seven-year-old alcoholic who fell downstairs, a forty-three-year-old epileptic who inhaled her own vomit, a fifty-nine-year-old heart attack victim, a forty-nine-year-old who died from alcohol poisoning and a forty-three-year-old drug user killed by pneumonia – all found days after they died. Whilst the rest of the country takes two weeks off, Busuttil's team are coping with an almost overwhelming tide of fatalities.

After the boy's stretcher clanked back down into the basement, an older man took his place on the slab. His chest was big and powerful with strange geometric shapes on it – 'the defibrillator,' said one assistant. 'He'd been off work for a few months with a damaged shoulder,' Busuttil read from his notes. 'On the Monday, he told one of his neighbours that he had indigestion pain in his chest and stomach and went out to buy some tablets. A few days later, the police found his body.'

The man's heart was almost 500 grams, way above the average weight of 240 to 360 grams. Out came his pancreas and the professor called me over. He pointed to some white, soapy spots in the dark red flesh. 'It's called fat necrosis. The pancreas is inflamed. His liver's enormous. This man is a heavy drinker, probably six pints a day. Maybe spirits. The heart's too big, and if you look at his arteries, they're damaged, furring up. It's arterial atheroma, which is Greek for porridge. The arteries were blocked and the heart had to pump extra hard to get the blood round, which is why it's so big.'

Although Busuttil's official report was laced with jargon, his basic finding translates as: this man sat at home and drank himself to death. 'Social services are not as good as they might be in terms of vulnerable people being visited often enough,' he shrugs. 'Resources are finite, the problem is becoming bigger, there are more demands not only on medical and social services but on everybody else. Mortgages have to be paid, the bills keep coming, there are more and more demands on people. We want cosy, complete lives and we want to look after ourselves rather than anybody else – even our families. If social services had more money or more staff . . . but they have to channel their resources into priorities.'

Priorities, of course. Where do you put finite resources? Well, you have a list. Some things are at the top and some things are at the bottom. And now the idea of priorities is suddenly in the air in a new and alarming way. There is the notion that smokers bring it on themselves, so perhaps we shouldn't spend quite so much money on treating them. George Best's doctor wished we could predict if an alcoholic would relapse before deciding to spend good cash on their liver transplant. At the core is the nagging idea that some people, basically, deserve to die.

If we took Busuttil's bodies and made a subtle switch – if, instead of finding seven neglected corpses on his table in one small city on one ordinary day he found seven dead children, or seven dead nursing mothers, or seven dead former models killed by stranglers in the woods – we might expect a different reaction. We might expect front pages and campaign groups and embattled government ministers appearing on the *Today* programme to promise legislation.

But then, it's not easy to stand next to an overweight forty-two-year-old man – a man who probably smells a little funny – and ask the public to care enough to save him. There's no glamour in the hacking cough of a bad-tempered alcoholic and no glory in placing your arms around a vicious junkie who pretends to be homeless. Jamie Oliver's ratings won't peak if he tries to improve the diet of a fat man living on tinned food and super-strength lager. Even the suicide . . . If I'd met him outside the morgue, a troublesome, aggressive kid who'd left school before sixteen and liked a drink and a row, would my heart have bled in the way it did when I saw the blue cord tight around his neck?

In 2006, Professor Pat Cantrill published a report on David Askew and Sarah Whittaker, a Sheffield couple who locked their starving children in excrement-smeared bedrooms while they spent benefit money on drink, state-of-the-art TV and computer games. The report blamed the low expectations social services and health professionals had of parents living in deprived areas. 'The factors that should have caused concern were known singly, sometimes collectively, to most of the services that knew the family, but their total impact on the welfare of the children was not thoroughly assessed or communicated between agencies and therefore not acted on,' Cantrill found. 'Seeking to defend inaction by stating that this family was one of many providing no level of care to their school-age children, and certainly not the worst, is not acceptable.'

These low expectations, this idea that the couple weren't quite as good at being parents as people with professional qualifications, allowed police, teachers and social workers to ignore a situation where maggots filled the nappy of a one-year-old child who was rescued hours from death.

Of course, a couple chomping takeaway pizza whilst shushing the kids so they can watch a DVD is not the tasteful face of deprivation. There is no *Road to Wigan Pier* nobility in such suffering. We have codified poverty as emaciation and rags. We want loneliness and despair to echo with a certain Victorian romance. We don't want to help someone who is one step removed from a chav. These people eat too much and watch TV; they ought to know better; they should do something about it. They are the undeserving poor.

If you can judge a society by the way it treats its most vulnerable, what can you say about one that would prefer not to notice them, that sees the vulnerable as somebody else's problem? Interestingly, Busuttil rarely sees non-white bodies in his suite – and those who do end up there are almost always victims of crime. He believes it's because the idea of community is still strong in Edinburgh's Asian and Chinese populations. The white majority, however, care less for their friends and family and are more prepared to let the undeserving fall by the wayside as we march on to an Ikea-designed vision of reasonably priced prosperity.

If Orwell returned to find out how we'd behaved since he wrote his book, we'd have to shuffle awkwardly and explain that, these days, the poorer you are the more we dislike you. We see the poor as irritating, ignorant and incompetent. And we as individuals, as professionals and as a society are turning away. The consequences can be fatal, not just for the heart-attack victim on the slab, not just for Sarah, stolen away from her hostel, but for the children of people who could easily be our neighbours.

The best we can do is to drug them – legally and illegally. According to figures obtained by the *Guardian*, swathes of northern England are prescribed antidepressants at far higher rates than even deprived areas in the southeast. Blackpool, Gateshead, Redcar and Cleveland have around three times as many antidepressant prescriptions per patient per year than Kensington and Chelsea – the area with the country's lowest prescription rate. Prescriptions in those primary care trusts, per 100,000 population, ranged from 133,829 to 120,137 in 2010.

And then there's self-medication. In 1936, the vice was drink; today, there's a smorgasbord of Class A chemicals. There's not much of a social class difference in drug use – about 7 per cent of sixteen to twenty-four year olds have taken drugs, according to the British Crime Survey, and they come from a broad and nationally representative demographic spread. The difference is in drug abuse. Just as with alcohol, it's working-class kids who die. Heroin users tend to come from areas of deprivation – even though only 1 per cent of sixteen to twenty-four year olds have taken the drug, its impact is huge.

Cheryl, a friendly Scouser, introduces me to her partner in a café at the edge of Toxteth on a cold, bright day. He's from Norris Green and ran with a gang of eight mates – nothing naughty, just pushing the buzz. Twenty years ago they tried their first joint, passing it between them and laughing when one seemed nervous. Today, he says, 'two are dead, two are in prison, two are on methadone but have jobs and then there's me and my mate and we're fine'.

He calls up clips on his mobile phone – an ersatz broadcast network, with footage of stolen cars revving, tribute graffiti to nineteen-year-olds shot dead in feuds and footage he'd been sent of a trapped heroin addict being baited like a bear. She was a youngish girl, possibly mid-twenties although it was hard to be sure. He said an old lady had dropped something into the post box and, presumably because she thought there was money in the envelope, the girl stuck her hand in through the slit to pull it back out.

Somehow her hand got stuck, the boys circled, pulled out their phones and started taunting her. 'Junkies are scum,' he said. 'Heroin washed the estates in the seventies and the eighties but these days it's all cocaine and skunk.'

Tim is a recovering junkie – unaware that he's becoming unfashionable. He's edgy and watchful, but pleasant company and laughs a lot, almost by way of nervous punctuation. He started using in his hometown of Keighley when he was twenty-two – 'Because there were nothing to do at all, no work, nothing, just hanging about with people,' he explains. 'They were using, which led me to using. I thought I'd never get a habit like you do but.' He laughs again. 'In a week or something I were messed up, having to use it to just feel normal. I was wanting to get out of it but, not being able to, that's part of it. Self-destructive.'

Edie, from Longside in Manchester, explains her addiction in rational terms. 'You know when you wake up in the morning and think it's school and then remember it's Saturday and you're warm in bed and don't have to get up and it's blissful? That's how it felt to me. So why wouldn't you feel like that instead of sitting in a cold flat by yourself? I'm clean now and I try to build my life back up, but there's a process I've got to go through – I can't just stop drugs and straightaway be all right and get a job and that. And it's always there.'

Tim's switched from methadone to Subutex – 'I'm trying to reduce on that, so hopefully . . . I don't want to use ever again, I'm sick of that.' A laugh. 'Waiting on street corners and everything, it's no good is it?' Another quick laugh. He moved to Bradford to help kick the habit – new faces, new places – and goes to the Bridge Project, a local drug treatment charity. He does a lot of training courses and works on allotments run by another charity, Keyhouse – the fruit and veg he helps grow goes to a homeless hostel in Keighley and he likes the idea of sending fresh food back to his hometown now he's clean.

'But they're finding it hard helping me get an apprenticeship. Because I'm twenty-nine they say these apprenticeships are for twenty-four or twenty-five year olds. The government keep saying they want people off drugs and get them into work but there's nothing to do. Most people who are like me who have had a drug problem – they've got to be in their late twenties, early thirties looking for opportunities and there's virtually nothing out there.'

He's also moved into a one-bedroom flat – it's clean and tidy, although has no carpet and the walls are stripped bare. There are a few basic sticks of furniture and a TV. He apologizes that he can't play any music, because he can't afford a stereo yet. We look at the bare walls. 'It's all right, just need to sort it out,' he smiles. 'I've applied for them community care grants, that's supposed to help you out if they've got you in a place and they always reject me. I've never had one in my entire life. You'd think they'd help you out at least once wouldn't you?' Another laugh. 'Having a drug habit and that, I weren't able to do it for ages until I got clean and I had a bit saved up.'

He wants the flat to work out because he's been clean for a while now. He had a mate stay over who was still using and it briefly got him back on to the drug. 'I had to boot him out,' he smiles slightly this time. 'I've got no willpower sometimes. I've gone round to someone's house and they've used in front of me and I've gone and used myself.' He laughs a rattling, empty Morse code of clipped white noise. 'That's why a lot of couples fall back if one uses . . .'

But – of course – the cuts are stacking the odds against him. Ian Guest at South Yorkshire Credit Union fears the changes to housing benefit where single people under thirty-five can only rent a room in a shared house will be 'horrendous – we have recovering drug addicts and actual addicts. You don't mix the two. If one bad apple upsets the others then you've got a madhouse. If you're trying to make a go of it on your own, living with three or four strangers it's easy to slip back into drugs or alcohol – not everyone, of course, but it is a reality because there's no work. People are bored to death.'

Tim's also just lost his disability benefit. By spring 2014 everyone on Incapacity Benefit, Severe Disablement Allowance and Income Support paid on the grounds of illness or disability will have been assessed for a new benefit – Employment and Support Allowance (ESA), introduced in 2008 by the Labour government. According to the DWP, 'people who are capable of work will move onto Jobseeker's Allowance, people who need more support while they prepare for work will get that help on Employment and Support Allowance and those people who are most disabled or terminally ill will get the extra support they need on ESA.'

The problem is, explains Oxfam's Moussa Haddad, deciding who's sick and who's not was taken away from the family GP back in 2005 and contracted out to Atos Healthcare – a French IT company. How did a French IT company get to rule on the health of Britain's sick? Because it invented a computer programme that can do the job cheaper and quicker than the patients' GP. The Logic Integrated Medical Assessment (LiMA) takes doctors through the examination. As well as prompting them to ask and enter relevant information, LiMA provides 'intelligent support' by identifying 'logical outcomes'. At the end of the assessment, LiMA suggests the outcome – sick or not. If the doctor disagrees they must override the system and justify doing so.

In February 2011, the *British Medical Journal* sent one GP – Margaret McCartney – to an Atos recruitment session. She found the experience disturbing. 'The message from the recruitment evening was quite clear,' she wrote. 'We were told: "You are not in a typical caring role. This isn't about diagnosing." And: "We don't call them patients . . . We call them claimants."':

Doctors work a minimum of four sessions a week and are paid 'per item' – £35.16 for an incapacity benefit examination and £51.37 for non-domiciliary disability living allowance (DLA) examination. The application forms state '10 DLA domiciliary visits cases per week would earn £40,211.60 per annum. Five LCWRA/LCW [limited capacity for work related activity/limited capacity for work] cases per session, for six sessions per week, would earn £62,883.60 per annum.' . . . The average morning or afternoon session should consist of five assessments, and it was made clear at the recruitment evening that clinicians who did not achieve this regularly would be picked up quickly on audit trails and speed of work addressed.

In August 2011, the General Medical Council (GMC) told the *British Medical Journal* that seven doctors working for Atos were under investigation. Two have already been taken by the GMC to an independent panel for adjudication on their fitness to practise. Over the summer, the chief executives of mental health charities Mind and Rethink Mental Illness, alongside consultants for the Royal College of Psychiatrists and the Centre for Medical Health, wrote an open letter to the *Guardian* saying there had been cases where people with mental health issues have taken their own lives following problems with changes to their benefits after an Atos exam. People suffering extreme mental illness, multiple sclerosis and even awaiting open heart surgery have been registered as fit to work. At around the same time the government announced that another £1 billion of NHS services will be offered to private companies, in services such as mental health and children's wheelchairs.

Which is why Douglas Hold is taking early retirement. 'I think that the reorganization of the health service is a complete nonsense,' he says, sighing. 'I really believe they don't know what they are doing. They are driven by dogma. We'll have a new model public institution, apparently remaining intact but actually an empty shell commissioning services from private corporations. Although there are some younger GPs who see it as a business opportunity I think it's inevitable that things would cost more. I don't want to be part of it.'

If, as a leaving gift, he could bestow one wish on his patients, what would it be? He thinks long and hard. 'People do seem to be drawn towards a lifestyle that is destructive for them. My patients are decent, ordinary people struggling in a way that we all are. No different from anyone else really. If they don't have a routine imposed on them by a job then it's easier for them to slide. There are some young guys who are fit, they go running, they play football, they may box and they look after themselves.

'But I suppose these days, young people always have

to come to terms with the drugs that are around, whether it's cigarettes, alcohol, weed, coke, speed or whatever. Nobody is immune from it and the influences are there on everyone. But what I have found is that people who are employed will tend not to drink so much or they will tend to use certain drugs – less harmful drugs. I suppose having a job and responsibilities can mitigate against the effects of alcohol, tobacco or other drugs. So if I could wish for anything, I suppose I would wish for employment. Jobs. Just that.'

CHAPTER 7

Dark Satanic Mills

Notice that the picture I have called up, of a working-class family sitting round the coal fire after kippers and strong tea, belongs only to our own moment of time and could not belong either to the future or the past. Skip forward into the Utopian future, and the scene is totally different. Hardly one of the things I have imagined will still be there. In that age when there is no manual labour and everyone is 'educated', it is hardly likely that Father will still be a rough man with enlarged hands who likes to sit in shirt-sleeves and says 'Ah wur coomin' oop street'. And there won't be a coal fire in the grate, only some kind of invisible heater. The furniture will be made of rubber, glass, and steel. If there are still such things as evening papers there will certainly be no racing news in them, for gambling will be meaningless in a world where there is no poverty . . .

George Orwell, *The Road to Wigan Pier*, 1936

Of course, there are areas of acute economic desperation where no riots happened. The overwhelming majority of people living in poverty had nothing to do with these events. But it is clear something has, and is, going wrong in our communities. Through our research, we know that people in some places feel absolutely powerless. And we know that many feel little loyalty to or involvement in their communities. We know that they believe their aspirations are frustrated and that whatever their effort they will not be recognised. People are worried about living in a culture that has increasingly defined status through material possessions and the accumulation of possessions as worthy in its own right. We know about the devastating effects of recession on communities – with some never coming out of recession. None of this excuses or even explains rioting, and it certainly does not give us a clear direction for preventing riots in the future – but it does emphasise the urgent need to tackle these social problems head-on.

Julia Unwin, chief executive, Joseph Rowntree Foundation, August 2011

I stayed one night in a small hotel in Bradford and fell into conversation with Neil, the stocky, good-humoured manager who looked to be in his late fifties but whose tales of Bradford suggested he was at least ten years older. Neil had travelled the world for years as a qualified referee – overseeing games from Nepal to the Ukraine. 'Bradford – we're an internationally minded city,' he explained. 'It's the mills. We'd be more likely to be trading with the rest of the world than London.'

As we chatted, the young man sitting next to me at the bar – Alan – joined in. Both proudly recited the oft-quoted statistic that – once upon a time – Bradford had more Rolls-Royces per capita than any other city in the world. Alan worked at a call centre – a numbing job with no significant chance of promotion. 'Without a degree you're just answering phones, whatever job title they give you,' he grumbled. One thing he was clear on, though – things were better in a call centre than in an old Bradfordian mill.

'The thing about mill work is that it's boring,' he explained. 'You, me, anyone would get bored. So we imported mental degenerates from the east who could sit in a mill, do the boring work and not mind. The only problem was, the mental degenerates started breeding.'

His casual racism came as a sharp slap in the face after his cosmopolitan tales of travel and ambition.

Neil, who'd been unhappy at the general state of integration in Bradford barely half an hour earlier, was horrified. Both men spoke at once, to me, the outsider, trying to define Bradford's view of race and immigration.

In Bradford, everyone seems to be wrestling with their own sense of how best to deal with the problem – conversations about race break through within minutes. Orwell dismissed it in *The Road to Wigan Pier*: 'All nationalistic distinctions – all claims to be better than somebody else because you have a different-shaped skull or speak a different dialect – are entirely spurious, but they are important so long as people believe in them.'

In Bradford, everyone will tell you they aren't racist, then mention the Asians or the whites or the Eastern Europeans but – unlike any debates I've witnessed on immigration in pubs, TV studios or earnest pages of print – the fundamental position seems to be that Bradford's citizens understand each other, and the problem, in a way that outsiders like me never can.

Perhaps this is because the city has known immigration since at least the 1840s – from County Mayo and Sligo in Ireland, the Jewish merchants who built Little Germany in the nineteenth century, then Poles and Ukrainians before the waves of Asian millworkers in the 1950s.

The people of West Yorkshire even gave Gandhi a

warm welcome when he toured the area in 1931 – an
unexpected reaction as he was organizing India's
boycott of cotton goods at the time and it was hitting
the area hard. Several thousand people gathered to
meet him at Darwen in Lancashire – so many that he
couldn't get off the train and had to dismount in
nearby Spring Vale instead. He stayed for a few days at
Heys Farm Guest house in West Bradford, spoke at
schools and met unemployed millworkers and a
deputation from the Clitheroe Weavers' Association.

Curiously, by taking the road to New Zealand, Alan
had followed waves of post-war Bradfordians – 'ten
pound poms', they were called – who's fares were
subsidized by an Australian government keen to keep
its population white and hold back a perceived tide of
Asian immigration. The slogan was 'populate or perish'.
For men from Bradford it presented a sweet opportunity. They'd come back from the front line in the
Second World War, where they'd shouldered responsibility and overthrown a skilful, mechanized enemy.
Returning to jobs sweeping mill floors was a dim,
unpleasant prospect. Australia and New Zealand had
sheep by the truckload and the miller's skill was in high
demand.

The irony scarcely needs pointing out. Millworkers
travelling to Australia to keep out cheap Asian labour
meant cheap Asian labour arriving to take unwanted
mill jobs in Bradford at the time the textile industry was

restructuring. There was new investment, but mill owners didn't want to spend unless they knew they'd get a fast return. This meant a cheap, relatively low-skilled workforce that was happy with long, antisocial shift and weekend work. South Asian immigrants met these demands more readily than locals – who were not only in short supply but had higher expectations in terms of wages and conditions of service.

The city has known race riots since the mid-1970s, usually thanks to the far right's intense interest in its ethnic mix. In 1981, the National Front petrol-bombed Asian homes. The Bradford police, however, arrested twelve Asian men and charged them with making and storing petrol bombs. The twelve pleaded self-defence and a largely white jury found them all not guilty.

Gary Cavanagh, a local journalist and author of *Bradford's Noise of the Valleys* – a history of Bradford's music scene – covered most of the disturbances. In 2001 he watched as right and left faced off in the town centre during yet another far-right march. 'Some neo Nazis kicked off down Ivegate and then all the kids got pushed up into the top of town and back into Manningham,' he remembers. 'I saw Asian kids kicking buses and older Asian guys shouting, "What are you doing?" It was like the youth just needed an excuse. They didn't go looting shops or owt. They were kettled into their own area and they ended up throwing petrol bombs. You could see them lobbing them from up the road. There's the cops with shields and then there's bricks and it was like a scene out of . . . it was a weird night because you never knew what was going to kick off.

'We were outside a club, drinking and smoking all night, just to see if owt came back down town but they'd kept them in Manningham where they'd ended up burning down that BMW showroom and nearly killing people in the Labour Club. It was all a bit crazy. I knew two lads who were out on the riots. One of them played football with me. He was only out looking for his younger brother but he got caught making that sort of movement, like he was waving or throwing something and he got caught on camera. He got sent down for two years. He had kids as well. They were really harsh on the sentencing to make a point.'

Cavanagh, like everyone I spoke to in Bradford, felt that the riots over the summer of 2011 had been different – less justified. For instance, Ateeqa felt the grievances in 2001 were triggered by harsh police stop-and-search tactics using counterterrorism as a cover for brutality. 'After Stephen Lawrence's murder the tone of the debate was about the rights of black people and the responsibilities of those in power,' she argued. 'After Bradford it was about the responsibilities of citizens and rights of those in power.'

Another woman, Eileen Turpin, an elderly white woman, felt Bradford's Asian kids had a reason to protest – though she wept as she insisted the government preferred Asians to the Bradford whites. 'Treat us equally,' she said, tears running down her face. 'That's what they should do but they're not.' She saw Asian families with stylish cars and designer labels and felt derelict and forgotten. 'What have we got? We've lived here, we've worked, we've got nothing. I get my clothes from the second-hand shops because I can't afford to buy owt new.'

She reminded me of the moment this book began as an idea – during a chat in a pub with my friend, Undaleeb – who was working for the 1990 Trust researching poverty in Britain's ethnic communities. It was clear that – by absolute measures – migrant workers, asylum seekers and immigrants had the worst of every possible world. One had lost both legs in a vicious beating at the hands of the Syrian police, another had been co-opted into a woefully underpaid labouring job sleeping four to a room and working twelve-hour shifts for half the minimum wage. They knew they were treated with suspicion and sometimes hatred, but they were also grateful and filled with hope. Almost none of them thought they were in poverty, despite having nothing.

What struck Undaleeb was that, in most cases, the white working class seemed the most isolated, the most desperate and the loneliest group.

In November 2011 the Joseph Rowntree Foundation

published the results of an enormous four-year project researching white working-class council estates. The Foundation found:

> a sense that local authorities 'washed their hands of us', as a woman in Thetford, Norfolk told a researcher. For the interviewees, evidence of such abandonment is expressed in the failure to adequately maintain local authority housing; when amenities such as sports and community centres are not maintained or replaced when unfit for use; and, importantly, in the failure to 'stand up for' local white working-class people in relation to minority groups.

The Foundation's researchers, however, didn't feel that the people on those estates were innately racist. They were struck by how many white people insisted they weren't racist – and who countered the accusation by insisting that those making that claim were simply being politically correct. At which point, many of them would recognize the stalemate they'd fallen into and say, simply, that – in modern Britain – the conversation on race has been shut down.

Bradford's complex and evolving attitudes to race illustrate this perfectly. I met Asian political activists horrified that the Asian community could spit the same venom against Eastern Europeans that it suffers itself. I met white working-class Brits who defined 'us and them' as being the people on their estate versus everyone else. The biggest frustration in Bradford amongst those that felt most strongly about immigration was that Bradford-born Asians were getting rich, not through benefit scams but through the shops factories and food plants Asian entrepreneurs created when the mills shut their doors. Of course, some of these entrepreneurs are as visibly rich and potentially annoying as their white predecessors, who were so bitterly scorned by Orwell:

> The type who starts off with half a crown and ends up with fifty thousand pounds, and whose chief pride is to be an even greater boor after he has made his money than before. On analysis his sole virtue turns out to be a talent for making money. We were bidden to admire him because though he might be narrow-minded, sordid, ignorant, grasping, and uncouth, he had 'grit', he 'got on'; in other words, he knew how to make money.

Most of the Asian entrepreneurs made the best of a terrible situation. Which isn't that unexpected. If you or your parents were the type of person who would travel the world in search of opportunity, you're more likely to be entrepreneurial. If, on the other hand, your grandfathers and fathers had always walked from a basic schooling to the pit or the mill or the factory, then you might not find education, creativity and enterprise at the heart of your family identity. And why should you? You had a job, your family and your friends around you so there was money, love and security right on your doorstep.

This would be fine if there was some wage equality. Of course, immigration flows from poor nations to rich. The time to panic is when immigrants choose to go elsewhere. But there are rich countries where a steady flow of immigrants creates little resentment because there are skilled jobs with decent salaries for all.

'Japan has very low immigration, not just because of its immigration controls but because there are hardly any jobs at the bottom,' Danny Dorling argues. 'You can't turn up and do an unskilled job because they don't have unskilled jobs.'

But here, with an education system stuck in the nineteenth century, the odds are stacked against you even if your family does treasure ambition and adventure. OECD figures published in June 2011 showed deprived pupils from Estonia, Indonesia, Latvia, Liechtenstein, Mexico and Slovenia as well as most developed nations exceed expectations for their social class more frequently than Brits. On average, the OECD found, 31 per cent of disadvantaged pupils educate their way up the social ladder whilst in the UK the proportion slumps to 25 per cent – placing us below the global average and thirty-ninth out of sixty-five nations.

The media often portrays immigrants as welfare cheats and benefit scroungers, as if you'd pay all the money you could save and borrow to a bunch of people-smuggling gangsters then place your family's life in their hands in the hope of securing a two-bedroom flat in a failed mill town where your state hand out would barely cover your food and fuel bills. Some of the people I met resented immigrants for something else entirely – for being excessively hardworking, for being low-cost employees, for building thriving small businesses then looking after each other, for respecting traditions and, perhaps most of all, for their mobility, both geographic and social.

The white working-class people who I met approved of these values – whatever the media thinks of Britain's working class, they believe in hard work, fairness and a sense of community. But they feel that all these things are slipping into the past. Blaming 'chavs' for being lazy and racist and motivated solely by bling isn't just inaccurate – it's one arm of the middle class blaming people for the things done to them by another arm of the middle class.

According to the Joseph Rowntree Foundation:

There is a danger that policy-makers turn to 'blaming' their target communities, whereas the fault lies primarily with those developing and implementing policy with limited understanding of community dynamics, and without proper consideration of the likely impact of the policy.

The diminishing availability of local authority housing stock, for instance, is explained by the reduction in housing brought about by the right-to-buy scheme since the early 1980s, and the requirement on local authorities to prioritise access by needs rather than residence. These changes in policy have led to extended families finding it difficult to remain in close proximity to each other.

So the worry about transient communities, about people bussed in at the whim of some external power, extends to concerns about nasty families from nearby cities dumped next door at the whim of a council and yuppie commuters snapping up the best property but rarely bothering to meet the neighbours. It's not – at heart – about colour or creed. It's the worry that the new lot – white or brown, rich or poor – don't care about this piece of land and will wreck it or ignore it however they please. It's about what will happen to the community. And then, worst of all, it's the feeling that those people are doing far better than you. It's the fear of being left behind.

The Joseph Rowntree Foundation's report kept returning to the word 'community' – people living in fear, having their jobs taken away, their benefits threatened, their housing stock diminished, their playing fields sold off and their opinions ignored. The people the researchers met feel that their traditional virtues of hard work, self-reliance, responsibility and independence are of little use when faced with these relentless changes. Community spirit is something they remember from childhood – a mythical era that's long gone.

In part, they're right. Reading Orwell's chapter on British cities today, you notice the loss of community – how there were always people on the streets, packed into pubs, holding meetings in the town square. Today you notice the isolation, the loneliness, the empty streets, the parents struggling with shame as well as poverty, the debts with BrightHouse in order to buy, not to share.

Admittedly Orwell is almost patronizingly senti-mental:

> I have seen just enough of the working class to avoid idealizing them, but I do know that you can learn a great deal in a working-class home. In a working-class home – I am not thinking at the moment of the unemployed, but of comparatively prosperous homes – you breathe a warm, decent, deeply human atmosphere which it is not so easy to find elsewhere. I should say that a manual worker, if he is in steady work and drawing good

wages – an 'if' which gets bigger and bigger – has a better chance of being happy than an 'educated' man. His home life seems to fall more naturally into a sane and comely shape. I have often been struck by the peculiar easy completeness, the perfect symmetry as it were, of a working-class interior at its best. Especially on winter evenings after tea, when the fire glows in the open range and dances mirrored in the steel fender, when Father, in shirt-sleeves, sits in the rocking chair at one side of the fire reading the racing finals, and Mother sits on the other with her sewing, and the children are happy with a pennorth of mint humbugs, and the dog lolls roasting himself on the rag mat – it is a good place to be in, provided that you can be not only in it but sufficiently of it to be taken for granted.

In Orwell's north, there's no mention of domestic violence – Mother is happy to sew and he writes that even when men are out of work they don't help with housework, because it is seen as being women's work. Although, as Stephen Ingle points out; 'Orwell didn't have any heroes, but the figure for which he had most respect was a working-class mother – forearms red with washing, big and burly, brought up children, brought up grandchildren, all that kind of thing. That really was, in his view, what civilization depended on.'

That version of community can be dangerous to those within, but also to those without. Community includes a modicum of defence. Asian kids in Bradford hid petrol bombs to defend their community. In Gin Pitt village, near Wigan, damaged families were bussed out from Salford and placed in local social housing some ten years ago. The fourteen-year-old kids especially became a menace, hanging around the ends of certain roads, insulting people, scrawling graffiti. Eventually, as the men at the Miners Welfare Institute say proudly, 'a couple of doors were kicked down and a couple of parents were told and that was that. They moved on soon after.'

Or take Barnsley. Under one of New Labour's community cohesion initiatives, two consultants charged with building said cohesion were hired for two days a month and paid £750 per day. They did warm, fuzzy things like asking children at local schools what they wanted the area to be like, and compiling a 'book of dreams' based on their answers. Richard in Dearne Valley went to some of their meetings and remembers one where they were discussing bringing the allotments back.

'There were the two guys from the agency, a guy from the council, a bloke from the local allotment association, a bloke who'd been around the councils funding sector and a local pub landlady, quite a big name,' he recalls. 'She wanted to talk about asylum seekers half the time, but mainly it was what are we going to do about this small mining town? They have all the problems of a rural location – isolation, poor public transport, poor local services, poor infrastructure – plus all the problems of an urban environment and none of the benefits of either. There were lots of overgrown allotments with broken fences and that seemed to be one of the possible answers. What happened next sort of summed up what's been going wrong.

'The man from the allotments association said there was a waiting list for allotments but people didn't want to clear the ground and fix the fences – they wanted the council to send someone over to sort it out. The council said they couldn't afford it. The money whizz – who knew his way around public-sector funding – said you need to get somebody who really knows about horticulture. The man from the allotments got quite cross.'

'We do really know about horticulture, don't tell me about horticulture, we've won every prize in South Yorkshire over the past ten years,' he shouted.

'No,' said the funding whizz, 'you need a horticulture champion.'

The allotment bloke just stared. 'What? What is that?'

'You need a Jamie Oliver of horticulture,' the funding whizz said.

'I don't,' said the man from the allotments association. 'I just want the fences mended and the ground weeded and I want the council to sort it out.'

'No,' said the funding guy, 'you need a horticulture champion so you can present horticulture as of therapeutic benefit – you can argue that it would help young offenders and the disabled and then you'll access all sorts of extra funding.'

'And then the rest of the meeting was about the height you'd need to have a flowerbed for adequate disabled access,' Richard says, sighing. 'The cost of the two guys from London's travel, accommodation and pay for that meeting would have been around £2,000. You could get two blokes on the minimum wage to clear the ground and fix the fences for that money.'

One of the consultants had parked outside a particular house on an ordinary street on his way to the meeting. On the way back, the next-door neighbour wanted a word with him. 'You can't park there,' a bulky man leaned out of his window. 'It's next door's parking spot.'

'There's no resident parking is there? I can't see any signs saying it's hers,' the Londoner replied, huffily. The bulky man opened his front door. 'You can't park there, it's next door's parking space, d'you see?' And the Londoner moved on hastily. Richard laughs, drawing the conclusion that community spirit was clearly strong in Barnsley, although the consultant would never understand he'd been scared off by the very thing he'd been paid to create.

There's always complexity to rivalry. Nogga Dogz

boys fight the Croxteth Crew in Liverpool even though some members went to the same primary schools. Labour MPs from Eton and Westminster shout down Tory and Liberal Democrat MPs from the same private school and the same university. Old boys' networks involve pack-style self-protection.

Ultimately, it's the scarcity of resources that makes communities scrabble for purchase. When the privileged riot, it's a bit of fun and they tend to get off lightly. In June 1987, for instance, one member of the exclusive Oxford student's dining society, the Bullingdon Club, smashed a restaurant's plate-glass window whilst celebrating the end of exams. Boris Johnson, Mayor of London, was a member at the time.

On 21 August 2011, the *Independent on Sunday* asked Johnson's spokesman Guto Harri what the Mayor of London remembered about the night and Harri admitted his recall included the name of the window smasher. When asked why Boris didn't reveal that name to the police – as he had felt 'blinding anger at the callousness and selfishness of the rioters' – Harri replied, 'That's neither here nor there. It is not my job to hand over a witness to the police to something that happened twenty-five years ago.' When asked why Boris had kept silent, he refused to answer.

Those MPs imprisoned for fiddling expenses included Eric Illsley, former MP for Barnsley Central, who pocketed £151,245 from the taxpayer and served four months of a one-year sentence for false accounting. Jim Devine, former MP for Livingston, fiddled £8,000 from the taxpayer, and was released after serving one-quarter of his sixteen-month sentence. David Chaytor MP, who fiddled £22,000, also served only one-quarter of his sentence. In August 2011, however, two teenagers who put up Facebook pages suggesting a riot in Warrington were jailed for four years each.

Orwell, despite his Eton education, would have cried 'class'. Eton currently has twenty old boys in the House of Commons, from Tam Dalyell to David Cameron. In total, twelve private schools are responsible for 10 per cent of British MPs. It's a sad reversal of the theory of British democracy – instead of a town or city or rural area clubbing together and deciding who should head down to Westminster to represent our interests, old school friends show up in the Houses of Parliament and send consultants out to tell us how they'd like us to run our communities.

Which may be why, despite the repressions and vested interests and demarcation and danger in Orwell's times, people along his Road who remember those days feel sorry for young people today. 'They won't get a job, the situation's never going to change and they'll die young,' one ex-miner told me, early in 2011 at Upper Morris Working Men's Club in Wigan. By the time I returned to Wigan in August 2011 the club had closed.

It had been repossessed in the middle of a bingo game. The players were told to finish their drinks and leave then and there. Most were retired, some in their sixties, and had been coming to the club all their lives.

If you were to grow up in Wigan now and think about the current merry gang of politicians – this clubby community that you had no chance of joining – what would you do? You come from a poor town with a lousy education and none of the contacts with which Ed Miliband, Nick Clegg or David Cameron were born. You might despair.

In the six months I spent writing this book, the only people under thirty I met who had a job worked for charities or the police. Everyone else was on short-term contracts, agency contracts, zero-hour contracts, training schemes or benefits. And they're cutting funding to charities and the police. You're going to find it hard to borrow money, and your support to find a job will be a brutally small carrot and violent stick. You'll be expected to move in search of work but to rely on your family – the family you left behind – to help you through hard times. And most of all, you'll need to consume though you have no money, no house and no hope.

'The people who rioted over the summer may have different reasons for being there and doing it,' argues Owen Jones. 'Some may have been angry, some may have been out for a free telly, some might have just been caught up in the moment. But if you look at who they are, they're people who don't have a future to throw away. They're largely young, unemployed and male and there's nothing on offer to any of them. It's having no future to lose that makes things dangerous.'

In Orwell's day, of course, there were no schemes or programmes. The community sorted many things out for itself. Whilst the welfare state was and is essential, it came with top-down decisions that, however well intentioned, inevitably alienate. Like the Sure Start centres designed with a loving, Scandic wood-and-leather trim that proved off-putting to young, white, single fathers – they assumed this was not a place for them and didn't get involved with the services on offer.

Previously, there were locally run associations, like the Upper Morris Working Men's Club, which were often rich in culture and creativity. Famously there's the Ashington Group, a branch of the Workers' Educational Association largely consisting of miners from the Woodhorn and Ellington pits. They started with art appreciation but gradually turned their hand to painting in their own right. In 1936, with Orwell nearby, the group held its first exhibition in Newcastle. In the 1940s they held exhibitions in London and worked with the likes of Julian Trevelyan and Henry Moore. Gradually interest waned and their meeting hut was knocked down in 1983. Their paintings hang in Woodhorn Colliery Museum and Lee Hall wrote a recent play, *The Pitmen Painters*, about them. These ideas of self-help died and our landscape is the poorer for them not painting it.

But, again and again, I found exceptions and examples that prove it doesn't have to be this way. Take Darlington Street, Scholes – the place Orwell begins the *Road To Wigan Pier*. Around 1997, Barbara Nettleton started the One Voice residents association. 'You want a nice place to live,' she explains. 'Fourteen years ago there was a flood of drugs into the area and a man was beaten to death in his house by druggies. We got together to build community spirit, get everyone together. We produced a newsletter, went door to door selling it and ran the association out of an office off a back street. We got burgled three years ago, a kid who had been working for us let his mates in. All the equipment was gone and the wall safe pulled out. We almost folded but all the other community and residents associations donated equipment, held benefit concerts, rallied around.' She smiles. 'It was nice . . .'

Ironically, one of the residents was a dealer. He paid every week, took his newsletter, came to meetings. One week, a car pulled up outside his house and emptied a machine gun in through the window. Barbara turned up at his house the following week and carried on collecting until he died of an overdose a few months later. Indeed, she seems immune from fear.

When they set up the association she told the *Wigan Observer* to print her name and address – she wanted the trouble now, not down the line. She's stood up in court giving evidence against kids getting ASBOs more times than she can remember, but no matter how bad the kids are she's never been threatened or insulted. For a while the police installed a red alert in her house just in case one of the ASBO kids came looking for her. At that time she had a cat and one night there was banging at both front and back door. The cops, like an armed response team, were outside both doors. Her cat had triggered the alarm. Over the radio link the controller had asked if she was OK and she hadn't heard. As there was no answer the police feared the worst. She had the alarm uninstalled shortly after.

The thing is, she explains, the neighbourhood is changing. Drugs are now just part of society. It used to be that you'd tell a kid off for drinking a can of Special Brew. Now there are nine-year-old kids thinking they're tough because their dad is inside for dealing. Old Mrs Smith has been replaced by a single mum struggling with kids and who can't see the point of £1.50 a month for a newsletter. Everyone still wanted the residents association when they had a problem, but how would that work? Providing help costs money and they couldn't charge £10 for each service on an à la carte basis.

And so Barbara set up Art to Art – a creative community resource centre in Sunshine House on Scholes Precinct, the shabby council-built shopping square near Wigan's few tower blocks. 'You need to keep people coming through the door but you need to be realistic,' she explains. 'This is an arts centre with a loyalty scheme. People belong and feel part of something. It costs £5 per year. Kids get one class free for every six weeks they attend, an adults one free lesson every ten weeks. They get a swipe card, and they can see the benefits adding up with each week of attendance. Membership's better because if you turn up at a class and it isn't what you want, you probably don't complain, you just leave. If you're a member, you complain or encourage. You feel you have a right to a voice.'

She keeps prices low – £3.50 – and some people come three or four times a week, often for the social aspect. There's an art exhibition every November. The first was three years ago and they barely had enough paintings to cover the wall. Last year 210 people attended the opening; they had to erect a marquee outside, sold loads of paintings and extended the show by four days.

A kids' show had just opened when I first visit. They turned Sunshine House into a cave so you had to crawl through tunnels to find children's drawings on walls. She hands me the exhibition booklet sporting a £1.50 price tag. I reach in my pocket but she laughs. 'It's free but if you put that sticker on it makes people feel they've got £1.50 worth of booklet for their £3.50 class.'

Andy from Allerton pops his head round the door –

a big ex-marine with tats and a crop who walks with a limp. He runs the centre's manga drawing class on Saturdays. They started with eight kids, then fifteen, then twenty-two. They've now extended over lunch into the afternoon and even through until dinner. A full day costs £3, a half day £2.

'Kids have to show work at the end of the morning or the end of the evening,' he explains. 'You can see their chest swell as they get a round of applause. There's isolated kids like Davy C. – bullied at school or at home, they sit in the corner and prefer not to work with others. They want to do their own thing. But he's getting better. He wouldn't speak at all at first. Now he does, although it's mainly to tell me he's all right and he'll do that bit in a minute.'

Barbara and Andy are both keen to stress this is not an after-school club. It's aimed at building a future. Alex, for instance, arrived six months ago – she's twelve years old, was vaguely interested in drawing but not what you'd call an artist. Now she's chosen design as a pathway at school. Her brother Oliver couldn't draw in any way – to be fair, he was only six years old – but now he's drawing robots and fire-breathing dragons with detailed trees and rocks in the background.

The organization is self-funding and has been since it started. It gets grants, but they have to be project grants so survival is hand to mouth. The chaos of grant applications takes up half their time. Adactus, the housing association, announced it had some money in July. Barbara raced to finish the form overnight but she was still waiting to hear in September. It's just £8,000 to work in five schools for a week each over twelve months, but it would help. 'When the mines and steelworks shut it meant the apprenticeships were taken away,' Barbara explained. 'You leave school without maths and English back then, you'd get an apprenticeship and learned a trade. Now there's nothing really.'

While she showed me her office – a small room with cluttered walls covered in wipe-clean timetables and hand-drawn cards – three policemen wandered in wearing their Kevlar vests, hats off and grinning. One of them threw a copy of the *Wigan Observer* on her desk with a grin. 'There you go,' he said. 'Take two minutes to read. Cover story.'

She read it, rolled her eyes and passed the paper over to me. 'Five Wigan men, including two police officers have been accused of involvement in a steroids case,' the lead story read. 'One of the officers, DC Paul David Fletcher, is also alleged to have leaked evidence to crooks.'

Fletcher was accused, the story said, of advising a man on bail for gun crime about the police investigation, gave another advice on getting a reduced sentence and a third information from police files. Fletcher denied cultivating cannabis but admitted supplying steroids to an undercover police officer – a particularly smart move for a detective constable.

The officers joked, flirted lightly in that way young men flirt with much older women and bought tickets for the Sunshine House lottery. One of the cops was new, so Barbara explained the rules. He took a ticket and said he'd pay next week.

After they left, she grinned cheerfully. 'I like them coming here, it sends a message,' she nods. 'There have been break-ins, but we've given the police keys so that when they're on their breaks on the night shift they can come in, make themselves a cup of tea and have their dinner. They take most of their breaks here now instead of heading back to the police station on the other side of Wigan. It means they're in the area for the whole shift. We keep a spare bonus ball in the lottery for the police to encourage them to enter – it means the police are invested in the centre. This is where they should police from – this should be part of their neigh-bourhood station.'

I'm briefly stunned. She's sixty-three years old, has lived through wars and strikes and has a mind so nimble that when she sees the old ways vanishing – the newsletter, the door-to-door residents association – she introduces swipe cards and lotteries, but with the same basic aim: to build and strengthen the community and to give people support and somewhere to turn. It seems to me, I say, that you're the Big Society in action.

She scoffs. 'Do you know why the Big Society won't work? Because it's planned from above, through councils and government departments. The big society should start on the streets. We should have kite marks for community centres like this – if we've got ten years of records and accounts they should give the money directly to us. They should let us set guidelines for education, because we know the area's needs and we know what it takes to get jobs. We could help create jobs, educate people, help them learn about their society and read and write. But no one wants that because they don't want a population of highly educated people all asking difficult questions.'

This is a shame because people everywhere fret about education but few do anything about it. Barbara ran a project called No Escape ten years ago in local schools, coordinating police, prisons, ex-prisoners, social workers, drugs charities, all explaining to kids what would happen if they bunked off school and got into trouble. Some schools she'd go to would have 16 per cent non-attendance at the beginning and she would leave them with 98 per cent attendance.

'These days we don't have the money to do it,' she explains. 'We're losing money hand over fist. We used to have a disabled morning on Mondays where their carers could learn how to use computers for £1 a lesson. Fortnight ago we were told the care homes no longer had enough staff to bring people. So people with learning disability can't integrate into the community.'

Everywhere – from unemployed miners in the Dearne Valley through ex-rioters turned charity workers in Liverpool to call centre workers in Sheffield to club promoters in Bradford to builders in Manchester – there's a common perception that kids' ambitions are unrealistic, that they all want to be reality TV stars or Premiership footballers and that they only want to be famous. One survey was quoted time and time again: in 2009, the top ten ambitions of children aged five to seven were sports star, pop star, actor, astronaut, lawyer, emergency services, medicine, chef, teacher and vet. Twenty-five years ago, those same ambitions were teacher, banking, medicine, scientist, vet, lawyer, sports star, astronaut, hairdresser and archaeologist.

'It's not just poverty, it's unrealistic dreams,' one person complained. 'Everyone wants to be famous for fame's sake. In Orwell's day, they didn't have the internet or fifty-seven channels. Kids today are unrealistic.'

Well, possibly. This survey was conducted by a PR company to mark the launch of a TV programme called *Tarrant Lets the Kids Loose* in which kids fulfilled their ambitions with a camera crew following them. Compare the list of ambitions in this heavily publicized survey with the regular survey by the Children's Mutual, a mutual society specializing – as the name might suggest – in saving for kids. Every year the Children's

Mutual conducts a similar survey of similar kids and produces very different results – although, to be fair, the message with each survey is that parents need to save for their children's future. With, say, the Children's Mutual.

In 2009, according to the Mutual, kids' top ten ambitions were teacher, doctor, vet, footballer, fire-fighter, actor, police officer, dancer, TV/cartoon character and hairdresser. In 2010 it was teacher, vet, footballer, doctor, firefighter, police officer, pop star, nurse, scientist and dancer.

What can we learn from this? Probably that – given kids include things like astronaut and cartoon character in their lists – they'd like to be something they've seen on TV and think looks quite fun. It's possible that – in the pre-teen years – no child is seriously thinking through their career plans. Perhaps these surveys teach us nothing, but do allow social commentators to despair at broken Britain and PR companies to get their clients in the papers.

I was wary of talking to children as I retraced *The Road to Wigan Pier* – Orwell didn't, Beatrix Campbell didn't in *Wigan Pier Revisited* in 1981 and it's unethical to quote them if they're under sixteen, without some fairly rigorous, properly monitored procedures. Anecdotally, however, I found the kids I chatted to along the way to be acutely and painfully aware of reality. They knew exactly how tight money was – if anything, they were more pessimistic than their reality required. They expected a potentially cataclysmic collapse was inevitably on its way. Many of them wished they had pocket money so they could give some to their parents and ease their mum or dad's worries. Many of them had grown up very, very quickly.

But while I was talking to Barbara, a mixed race girl, Olga was dropped off by her father. In a complex net of modern family relationships, her dad and mum had split and both remarried. Olga's dad was ferrying all the kids from both couples around to their classes and to their schools – today was the first day of term for some of them, including Olga. Her headmaster had given her permission to miss the first day so that she could complete a pencil-drawing course given by Art to Art. Today was the last day and she wanted to finish the work. Why did it matter so much? I asked her. She looked up, her eyes gleaming with the joy only a ten-year-old child can have: 'Because art's just brilliant. It's the best thing I've ever done.'

A few months later, on 18 November 2011, during my final visit to Wigan while researching this book, Art to Art's annual exhibition opened. The walls were crammed with paintings – over 200 artists restricted to just four pictures each. There was modernism, manga, cutesy kittens, dark images, graceful nudes, collage and even a stern portrait of Jesus with his cross. The mayoress came early and walked around, clearly stunned by the quality of the work. You could feel her attitude change – from professional town-hall worthy turning up on a Friday night at a community centre to do her duty and smiling politely, to one of admiration as Barbara walked her around the exhibition, showing off the work. The mayoress became a punter. Her speech was devoid of the usual platitudes. It tripped out awkwardly, unrehearsed, awed by what she saw all around her.

I had to leave early to catch the last train. As I slipped out of the door I took one last look at a room full of people who could paint so well, but who had never had the chance before and were filled with pleasure at what they'd created. All ages, shapes, sizes and colours – Britain at its best, believing in dreams.

On the way back to the station I walked past Wigan Pier. Or what they call Wigan Pier today. The Pier itself never really existed, in fact. The title is a reference to a music-hall song about first-class train passengers who mistake a coal jetty for a place of entertainment. There used to be a Wigan Pier Experience, but that too is closed now. The building's still there – waiting to see what comes next.

CHAPTER 8

The Lion and the Unicorn

It hardly needs pointing out that at this moment we are in a very serious mess, so serious that even the dullest-witted people find it difficult to remain unaware of it. We are living in a world in which nobody is free, in which hardly anybody is secure, in which it is almost impossible to be honest and to remain alive. For enormous blocks of the working class the conditions of life are such as I have described in the opening chapters of this book, and there is no chance of those conditions showing any fundamental improvement. The very best the English working class can hope for is an occasional temporary decrease in unemployment when this or that industry is artificially stimulated by, for instance, rearmament. Even the middle classes, for the first time in their history, are feeling the pinch. They have not known actual hunger yet, but more and more of them find themselves floundering in a sort of deadly net of frustration in which it is harder and harder to persuade yourself that you are either happy, active, or useful.

George Orwell, *The Road to Wigan Pier*, 1936

'Often you get asked – what would Orwell have thought about a particular incident, and I am inclined to take a coward's way out and say, "Well, find out what most of the left is saying and Orwell would have said the opposite,"' Stephen Ingle says, with a quiet smile. 'He is trying to combine old myths about Englishness with new myths about politics.'

In the second half of *The Road to Wigan Pier*, Orwell's solution to the problems he'd found was simple – 'the idea that we must all cooperate and see to it that everyone does his fair share of the work and gets his fair share of the provisions seems so blatantly obvious that one would say that no one could possibly fail to accept it unless he had some corrupt motive for clinging to the present system'.

As Ingle points out, however, Orwell goes on to argue that 'the worst advertisement for Socialism is its adherents'. And he proceeds to wade in to fruit-juice drinkers, nudists, sandal-wearers, pacifists, feminists and pullover-wearing intellectuals who read the *New Statesman*.

After he finished *The Road to Wigan Pier*, he put down his pen and went to fight in the Spanish Civil War in the name of democracy. He survived and, in 1941 with bombers overhead, decided we needed a specific, British social revolution.

'It will not be doctrinaire, nor even logical,' he argued. 'It will abolish the House of Lords, but quite probably will not abolish the Monarchy. It will leave anachronisms and loose ends everywhere, the judge in his ridiculous horsehair wig and the lion and the unicorn on the soldier's cap-buttons. It will not set up any explicit class dictatorship . . . it will never lose touch with the tradition of compromise and the belief in a law that is above the State.'

He concluded, with an apology to Scotland and Wales:

England has got to be true to herself. She is not being true to herself while the refugees who have sought our shores are penned up in camps, and company directors work out subtle schemes to dodge their Excess Profits Tax . . . Nothing ever stands still. We must add to our heritage or lose it, we must grow greater or grow less, we must go forward or backward. I believe in England, and I believe that we shall go forward.

In many ways, he was predicting the muddle of the

post-war system, where the wage gap narrowed, houses were built, jobs created, healthcare made free and, according to Rowntree, poverty vanquished – not through the crushing boot of ideology but through compromise and negotiation.

He was predicting the world that took Sid and Trevor Smith from a grubby news stand in an old arcade to a large house in a peaceful village, the system that carried the Hammonds from blacklisted troublemakers to prosperous judges, and the ideas that Gerry and Harry Kennan spent their lives struggling to protect.

Their home – Wigan – began as a mill town. Then, when we needed coal, it became a pit town. When we shut the pits, it managed to attract Hitchens and Heinz food processing plants. Now Heinz may leave and the council is shedding jobs. If you visit the war memorials in Wigan – or Liverpool, Manchester, Bradford, Barnsley – you see endless names of the dead – from the Great War, the Second World War, the Falklands, the Gulf . . . every time the country called, they answered. They answer still. The first time I visited Wigan in 2011 it coincided with a military funeral and the streets were filled with hard-drinking, grim-faced servicemen. In November 2011 I stood beside the war memorial in Wigan, saw the names of the fallen from the Falklands, saw the wreaths for the recently killed, saw the messages from children promising to remember their dead fathers. Watching amputees come home from Afghanistan, it's usually a council estate that receives them.

And so what more do we expect of Wigan? Dig for us, die for us – all of which the town has done, sometimes cheerfully, sometimes drunkenly, sometimes noisily. Economists are talking about redundant communities, towns that have no point. They were built on a coal seam, the coal is gone, so why are the people still there? Leave the city, abandon your home. If not, you have no one but yourself to blame.

Orwell's generation at least had the luxury of choosing from possible solutions to the problems he'd observed. In 1933 John Maynard Keynes published *The Means to Prosperity*, with the specific idea for tackling unemployment in a global recession, and his magnum opus *The General Theory of Employment, Interest and Money* came out in 1936 – the book that started Keynesianism. There were rivals and collaborators such as John Hicks with the *The Theory of Wages* in 1932 or J.K. Galbraith introducing the New Deal in the States. Marxism still had a tainted currency. In Spain, anarcho-syndicalism held sway in Catalonia. Brutal forms of nationalist economics in Germany and Italy appealed to sections of British society. And the classical ideas of Adam Smith were tainted but open for review.

Today, we only have one option – a globalized free market, once known as monetarism or Thatcherism –

and it's in trouble. 'What we are seeing is the structural crisis of Thatcherism,' argues Dr Johnna Montgomerie, economist at the Economic and Social Research Council's Manchester-based Centre for Research on Socio-Cultural Change. 'If the 1970s were the crisis of Keynesianism some thirty years after it came to the fore in politics then this is the same for Thatcherism – thirty years on, a structural crisis. Now is a time for radical thinking, for a new set of economic ideas.'

Danny Dorling agrees. He has been crunching his way through reams of raw data for the past fifteen years, building up a picture of poverty and wealth in contemporary Britain. In study after study, he uncovered numbers proving we've been living through an era of unprecedented widening inequality and declining social mobility and he expects that to get a lot worse.

I asked him how to compare Orwell's day with the reality of 2011. He thought for a moment, then said, 'For most people alive in Orwell's time, 1936 was wonderful compared to 1911. The infant mortality rate was three or four times lower, for instance. You could look at wages, look at health, look at everything and say – what was Orwell complaining about? Orwell should have said – right, we've got 1936. This is great. Let's have 1936 forever.'

He gave a sly grin. 'And you would never have free secondary education, you would never have a health service, you would never have inside toilets in council houses. Today you could say – this is one of the richest countries on earth, it's fine – the people cleaning up the coffee in the kitchen here will go home and have a widescreen telly. Or you could say, but in thirty years' time their children could live in a situation where they are happy with their work, they look forward to it, it's enjoyable and they've chosen to work. Could you imagine if everybody could choose what job they wanted to do?

'You can go even further; I've started to do work looking at the chances that our great-grandchildren could not have passports – just like our great-grandparents didn't. I know it can happen in one generation – partly because the population is going to dip. Wouldn't it be good if we could go round the world without a passport? And then you say – what would it take incrementally to get to that point? If people had been satisfied with their lot then, what a terrible world it would be now. If you look back at 1936, the people saying things were great would look stupid from today's context. That's the folly of saying things are fine just now. And they're clearly not fine just now.'

How could we do this? Suppose we could pull together a government of national unity to re-create the benefits of the post-war dream with imagination, egalitarianism, eccentricity, compromise and solidarity to imagine the world Dorling describes, what would we demand of it?

In September 2011 I spent an evening with people in Letchworth – the garden city Orwell praised and condemned in equal measure – talking about what they wanted for the future. From dyed-in-the-wool Tories to apolitical twentysomethings their ideas were very similar to the communities in Nelson, whose opinions were canvassed then roundly ignored – education, jobs, housing, safe communities, green spaces . . . nothing outrageous. Just something so that they didn't have to feel sorry for their children.

If you tell Trevor Smith's, Tony Hammond's and Gerry Kennan's stories to most people, they point out the value of the grammar school education Trevor and Tony received. Comprehensives take a lot of blame. But the secondary modern system was failing. Micky – the man who lives on mince and chilli to give his daughter clothes and a decent meal – went to Ashton-in-Makerfield Secondary Modern. 'I was a kid who got free school dinners and I did get the grant uniform,' he remembers. 'If you asked for something it was, "Well, let's see." You know? And really, ambitions were so low in our school – it was there to produce people to work in factories. Most kids left school and worked in a factory or the ambitious ones became cab drivers, window cleaners, drivers, porters. They were the jobs that we were qualified to do and that's no use today.'

Something had to change. If the comprehensive wasn't the solution, it's worth reflecting that, in some places, a great education is vital but only part of the story. Kate Reader went to Brooke Weston school in Corby – the former steel town that saw unemployment soar when the steelworks closed in 1981. Brooke Weston opened in 1991 as a city technology college, founded with the help of two businessmen – Garry Weston and Hugh de Capell Brooke. It has a radical syllabus – eight weeks on, two weeks off, swipe cards to sign in, lessons until 8 p.m. if students choose. The school's GCSE results are spectacular but, as Kate found, many pupils fail almost immediately afterwards.

'I had a friend, used to be so scared of her dad she'd flinch every time the door opened, who was the smartest kid I knew,' she explains. 'Really witty. Now she's signing on with a kid in a mucky estate. I got on to a degree at Sussex University and she came down with me at the start of the first term. You could see the world changing the further south you went. It was like a different country – these people who hadn't been afraid, who were kind and soft and charming, really posh people, I suppose. She was getting on the train back and she said she had no idea this was how some of Britain could be. She was really angry. If people don't know what they can dream of becoming, if all they know is a rubbish town, a violent town, then they don't hope for anything apart from a child who will give them unconditional love.'

One way to help Kate's friend escape her trap is with decent jobs. On the Road to Wigan Pier the idea of a job is long gone – and not purely in terms of unemployment. The proletariat has been replaced by the precariat – people working on zero-hour contracts or short-term agency contracts, with no job security, adequate income, protection against illness or political representation while facing rising debts and household bills. Professor Guy Standing at Bath University believes the precariat could make up 25 per cent of the UK.

Standing's vision of the future beats Orwell for its bleak dystopia. But where are the ideas that challenge his predictions? And what sort of country are we creating if we don't fight against that doom? What investment in your society do you have if you're just starting out and the best option you can see locally is a forty-five-year-old with reasonable skills wearing an orange apron saying 'Welcome to B&Q'? Effectively you're being told that if you are really good and work really hard you could be that person, wearing that apron. You can imagine a world in which you are paid a reasonable wage and the people coming in to buy stuff are only paid 20 per cent more than you, a world where you don't mind saying 'Hello, welcome to B&Q, can I help you?'

The government's current solution is to reduce job security rather than enhance it – give people on zero-hour contracts working for agencies fewer rights than before. They argue it's necessary for a thriving economy. Over in Manchester, Karel Williams disagrees. He's professor of accounting and political economy at Manchester University's Business School – but he also helps out at the Centre for Research on Socio-Cultural Change.

Williams has spent some time crunching numbers and believes we could rebuild our manufacturing base with a few simple ideas – and we could easily bring factories back to the northwest. He talks of manufacturing security – how, like food or energy supply, this should be an object of national policy. The country needs manufacturing because we simply cannot afford to import everything. Large factories could boost recovery by selling branded, finished products, spending on research and development, building a skill base and supporting suppliers.

It might take a generation to solve the problems that have built up over the past thirty years, but we could start by treating manufacturing as we currently treat the City, he argues. Every hedge fund and private equity firm now relies on tax accountants and corporate lawyers to advise on how to route its cash flows through tax havens so the partners can take out more profit. Why not socialize this model for manufacturing

– adjusting the tax regime and offering aggressive rebates and incentives for firms that deliver social benefits of output, investment and employment? Why not break with the generic low-tax, pro-enterprise policies and offer sector specific incentives in manufacturing for more focused purposes?

Of course, Trevor, Tony and Gerry also saw housing change dramatically – Tony remembers visiting a college girlfriend in the 1960s who didn't have running water. New housing problems replaced existing housing problems – with one clear lesson: listen to the community. The Broadwater Farm estate in north London – inspired by Le Corbusier – appears to offer nothing but a depressing response to this chaos. Building began in 1967. Ethnic tension, high unemployment, drug dealing, crime and heavy-handed policing – culminating in the death of Cynthia Jarrett during a police raid on her flat after her son was arrested with a fake tax disc – boiled over into a sprawling battle between police and youths on 6 October 1985. Police protecting firefighters were attacked. They withdrew but PC Keith Blakelock fell and was butchered with machetes.

After the riots, the Tory government invested heavily in Broadwater Farm – spending £33 million knocking down walkways and making structural improvements. Haringey Council installed a neighbourhood office. Residents paid up to £10 per week for a concierge system that reduced crime to virtually zero. Empty shops became light industrial units. The change was dramatic – in the first quarter of 1985 there were 875 burglaries on the estate. In the first quarter of 2010, there were ten. Broadwater Farm has the lowest rent arrears in Haringey and a lengthy waiting list for housing.

'The estate has been blessed, too, by a series of strong individuals who have made an important difference by devoting their lives to improving the estate,' argues Christian Wolmar, a journalist who covered the estate during the 1980s. 'Notably Clasford Stirling, a long-time youth worker who runs countless soccer teams and other activities for young people, and the experienced housing manager, Paul Dennehy, who goes well beyond the remit of his job, by turning up in the evenings and weekends for meetings and social events which, he says, is an essential part of getting the community to trust him.'

Twenty-five years later, rioting erupted again just 400 metres away on Tottenham High Road – again in a flare up over heavy-handed policing after officers shot Mark Duggan on 4 August 2011. Does that mean the community work was wasted? No, it means that people in Letchworth and Nelson know what they're talking about when they ask for what they need – education, jobs, housing, safe communities, green spaces. Clean the place up and plant a few trees, a few more police patrols, invest in sports and community facilities especially for the young and help create some good local jobs.

Of course, a decent education system, good-quality community-minded housing, plenty for kids to do and decent wages wouldn't cure all society's ills, but it would be a start.

Obviously, such a government isn't on the way. It should be – if only for Sarah D.'s sake. We all have our ideas, our beliefs, our goals and our theories but right now in this country people are dying from poverty-related illness and being snatched off the streets. In Westminster, on political blogs and in hysterical newspapers, there are points to be scored if you deliver a cunningly wrought and highly finessed debating phrase. But these are from people whose income is secure, who don't go to jail for their crimes, for whom debate is something esoteric with hands shaken afterwards because it was a jolly good time. Ed Miliband's wife and George Osborne's wife are best friends from university. You could be thinking they've been having a laugh behind our backs.

Tony Hammond, the son of the blacklisted communist miner who became a judge, is optimistic: 'There's a tradition of doing it yourself up here. The miners used to go home covered in filth but we helped change that. My dad was proud that he had helped get pithead baths built but often the miners had to fund them.' He shrugs. 'I think people tend to altruism. We can see unfairness. We might grumble but we do a good job. I just think we're badly served by our governments.' He sighs, then smiles, remembering his troublesome father, who raised his son so high. 'So we sometimes have to do it ourselves, and maybe now is one of those times.'

He's right in one way. I remember sitting in Barbara Nettleton's office in Wigan as she explained how you can build community on a swipe card and lottery system using art as the focus and be entirely self-funding – I could feel my mouth fall open. Over the previous months I'd been agonizing with all sorts of people from learned academics to earnest MPs to worried doctors and desperate charity workers about the vanishing sense of community across the country – the decline of great traditions and an irreplaceable loss and we'd despair. And then this sixty-three-year-old woman said – well, it's easy isn't it? Education, creativity and community. And she showed me just how easy it can be.

I remember driving through Manchester with Pete, delivering fresh food to those in poverty, his burly shoulders lifting sacks of potatoes, on first-name terms with lonely people, showing me how to get things done.

I remember Ian Guest at the South Yorkshire Credit Union telling me that one way to rescue thousands of families from debt would be to improve access to low-cost credit, which wouldn't hurt anyone and already exists.

Eileen Devaney in Speke knows that one way to address the problem of housing stock – with no homes being built, right to buy removing the best housing stock, soaring prices forcing young buyers off the property ladder, social-housing landlords exploiting everyone from single mums to migrant workers – would be very simple: 'you could start with the right to sell. If you could sell your house to the council when you wanted to leave an area they could replenish housing stock, and people fleeing shabby areas could get their money's worth, which means they wouldn't panic-sell and proper families could move in. It's easy, isn't it?'

In a real meritocracy, Ian Guest and Barbara Nettleton and Eileen Devaney and the team behind Herbie would be sent to Westminster to represent our best interests and I'd have faith that they'd do better than anyone there right now. I'd feel a whole lot safer about the future. Having watched these people stride through some of the roughest council estates I've seen, without fear or bodyguards or police protection, day after day to get the job done, I'm sure a few riots would be no problem whatsoever.

These people are all either volunteers or earning a pittance for what they do because they feel proud to help their community. If they get so much reward for bringing a tiny change to the place they were born, being a politician ought to be the most nourishing job in the world. Someone like Barbara Nettleton works 24/7 to serve her community – she has all the local councillors' home phone numbers and says that calling them at 11 p.m. is a great way of getting things done. By her example, MPs should be paid minimum wage and serve us for the pleasure of building a beautiful future for all.

It's the cleaning, the digging of coal, the building of houses – the jobs that the people mentioned in this book are doing for minimum wage on zero-hour contracts and struggling to survive – those are the jobs that should be hugely rewarded. Instead, each new bill brings less security – in housing and employment.

We need that to change. It's the least we can do to repay the debt we owe. As I write, there are protestors camped outside St Paul's cathedral – part of the Occupy movement that's sprung up in towns and cities across the world. One criticism of the protests is that they have no specific demands, just a general despair at the current system. If anyone from the Occupy Movement or even anyone from government wanted specific solutions about how to deal with the mess we're in, there are people waiting in the northwest of England with a whole list of practical solutions. All you have to do is ask.

Index